MODELING THE PAPER INDUSTRY

Jeff Wilson

DEDICATION

This book is dedicated to the memory of my colleague and friend Jim Hediger. Jim was an outstanding modeler who was interested in industries and loved sharing his knowledge of them and how railroads served them. His extensive photos were invaluable in doing this project. Jim, I wish you could have seen the final product — thank you. — *Jeff Wilson*

ACKNOWLEDGMENTS

Thanks to Cody Grivno, Keith Kohlmann, and Steve Smedley for providing information and photos for this book. I'm also grateful to the late Dave Ingles and his father, John, for their many photos of freight cars and trains from the late 1950s onward. — *Jeff Wilson*

On the cover: A Duluth & Northeastern 2-8-0 snakes through the winding trackage of a Cloquet, Minn., paper mill in 1963, pulling paper boxcars and a coal hopper between pulpwood cars (left) and Canadian National paper cars (right). The railroad was among the last to regularly use steam power in the United States. John Gruber

Opposite page: The Northern Pacific and other railroads often used gondola cars in pulpwood service. Trains Magazine collection

Back cover: Main photo: Several pulpwood loads head eastward from Superior, Wis., on the former Great Northern in the early 1970s. J. David Ingles **Inset:** A worker stands under the continuous paper sheet in the paper machine at the Mississquoi paper mill in Sheldon Springs, Vt., in 1941. Jack Delano, Library of Congress

Firecrown
405 Cherry St.
Chattanooga, TN 37402

Shop.Trains.com

Published in 2025
29 28 27 26 25 1 2 3 4 5

Manufactured in China

ISBN: 979-8-89491-021-5
EISBN: 979-8-89491-022-2

Editor: Rene Schweitzer
Book Design: Lisa Schroeder

CONTENTS

THE PAPER INDUSTRY OFFERS MANY MODELING POSSIBILITIES

A Cloquet Terminal crew switches cars next to the wood yard at the huge Sappi paper mill at Cloquet, Minn., in September 2009. The mill uses about 5,500 tons of wood per day. The Cloquet Terminal is the surviving remnant of the Duluth & Northeastern, a historic paper and lumber short line well known for operating steam locomotives into the 1960s. Steve Smedley

Railroads have been serving the paper industry ever since mills began large-scale mechanized paper operations in the mid to late 1800s. Railroads deliver raw materials such as logs, wood chips, chemicals, and fillers, and carry out carloads of newsprint, packaged products, and byproducts to customers throughout the North American rail network.

By the early 1900s, papermaking had become one of the largest industries in North America. Many smaller railroads counted paper (and related traffic) as their major revenue source; several short lines were owned partially or entirely by the paper mills that they served. Major railroads that served the industry devoted significant numbers of railcars to the traffic, with thousands of pulpwood and wood chip cars, plus thousands of boxcars assigned strictly to newsprint service.

Although this traffic has evolved significantly, with most pulpwood and chip traffic moving to trucks, railroads still haul a significant amount of paper, clay, and chemicals for the industry. The mills themselves, along with the serving railroads, railcars, and other details, make the paper industry an appealing one for modelers.

Paper mills are fascinating places, with a wide variety of buildings — many of them huge — housing wood-processing equipment, chemical pulping vats, papermaking machines, and serving as warehouses. Although all mills share common characteristics, no two are alike. Distinctive features include large wood lots, where pulpwood and chips are stored outdoors (with a variety of conveyors and cranes), a power plant, numerous tanks of many styles and sizes, networks of piping, and prominent loading docks for railcars and trucks.

Even in the steam era, paper mills were large. Modern mill complexes cover dozens of acres and can include miles of in-plant trackwork, with an on-site yard and multiple spots to load and unload various types of railcars.

Even if you don't have room to model a mill, there are many other space-saving options for capturing parts of the industry. Ancillary operations and businesses that can be modeled in tighter spaces include pulpwood and chipping load-out operations, which may take place hundreds of miles from the mill; paper customers, such as printing plants and urban newspapers; and packaging companies that rely on paper and cardboard to produce their products. Transloading operations also offer modeling potential, as large rolls of newsprint are often transferred from railcars to trucks for final delivery in cities. Many of these are very modelable, requiring just a simple spur or siding and some loading equipment and details.

A Mississippi Export GE 44-tonner pulls two chlorine tank cars and several other cars from the Southern Kraft Paper Co. mill at Moss Point, Miss., in 1941. The mill would later be purchased by International Paper Co. General Electric

You can model the railcars and traffic of the paper industry regardless of the region and era you model. Boxcars of newsprint and finished paper products can be found on almost any line in North America. Many of these cars have been distinctive, with labels, paint schemes, heralds, and stenciling indicating their specific service in carrying paper products.

Likewise, cars carrying chips and pulpwood — although more regional in nature — are quite distinctive, and have traveled over many railroads. Other traffic that can be modeled includes tank cars of kaolin clay, lime, and titanium dioxide slurry; covered hoppers of clay, starch, and other fillers and chemicals; hoppers of coal or tank cars of fuel (for in-mill power plants); and distinctive tank cars of many chemicals including caustic soda, hydrogen peroxide, chlorine, and sulfuric acid or molten sulfur.

We'll start with a look at the history of the industry and how it evolved and grew in the U.S. and Canada. We'll then examine the papermaking process, see how mills are designed, how various processes work, and how mills vary in size and appearance, then look at the railcars used for both raw materials and finished products. We'll finish by covering typical railroad operations at and around mills, then provide some tips for capturing the feel of prototype mills in model form.

Turn the page and we'll start by examining the history and basics of this interesting industry.

CHAPTER ONE

HISTORY OF THE PAPER AND PULP INDUSTRY

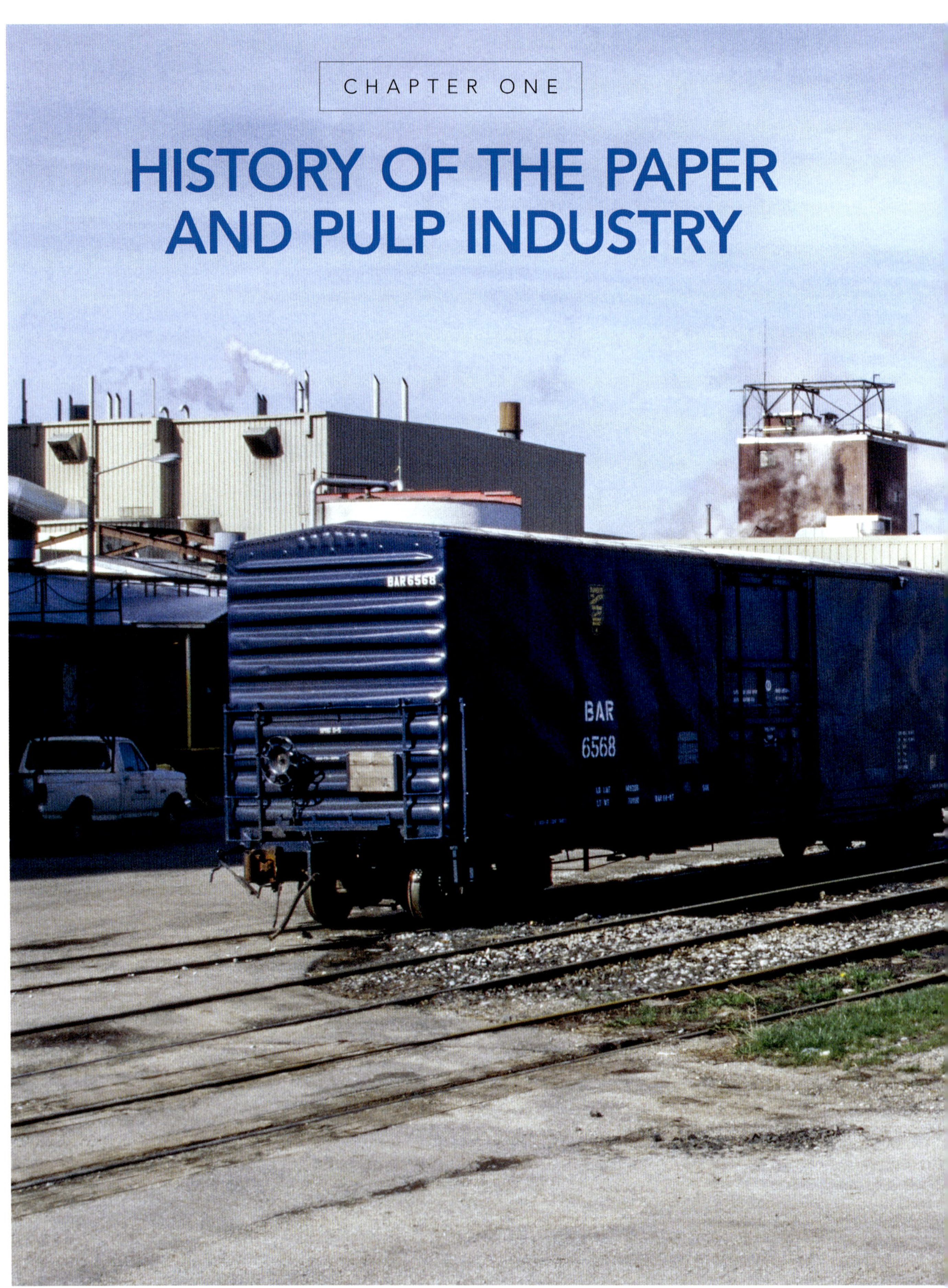

The paper industry incorporates several types of mills and industrial operations that process logs and wood chips into pulp, then transform the pulp into a tremendous selection of finished products. Newsprint, writing paper, tissue, and corrugated packaging are just a few of the products that emerge from paper mills.

Paper mills offer many appealing modeling features, including varied buildings, tanks, piping, and conveyors; multiple tracks throughout the complex with lots of railcar loading and unloading spots; semi trailers and other vehicles; and myriad detail opportunities. This scene is at a Menasha, Wis., mill in the mid-1990s. Jim Hediger

Railroads have played a role in the industry since the mid-1800s, bringing wood and other raw materials to mills, then delivering the finished products to customers throughout North America. The paper and pulp industry offers a wide variety of potential modeling and operational opportunities for model railroads, regardless of the era, region, or specific prototype railroad that you model.

Industry overview

The industry comprises two basic operations: making pulp from wood (including logs and wood chips, as well as recycled paper), and then taking the resulting pulp and making paper from it. Individual mills can do one or both processes; the factories that make both pulp and paper are known as integrated mills. We'll look at the specific processes and mills in depth, including how their operations (and those of the railroads that serve them) have evolved, in chapters 2 and 3.

The papermaking industry is huge: The market value of the North American pulp and paper market was more than $56.4 billion in 2023. The 202 paper and pulp mills in the U.S. (as of 2024) produce about 75 million tons of paper products annually, and the 46 mills in Canada add another 12.1 million tons (Canada exported $13.6 billion in paper products in 2022).

The global market for paper is volatile. Specific production numbers among paper-producing countries vary widely from year to year as demand for various products changes (an example is the shrinking demand for newsprint but an increase in demand for packaging cardboard). As of 2024, the U.S. ranks second in world paper production (behind China); Canada ranks 10th.

The paper market and the mill operations and markets of Canada and the U.S. have long been intertwined — especially for newsprint — with a lot of rail traffic crossing the border. We'll focus on these North American operations, looking at the mills, railroads, railcars, and operations in both countries.

All of this traffic has been a major revenue source for railroads, although it can be difficult at times to determine specific numbers and data regarding traffic and carloads. Pulp, pulpwood, chip, and paper traffic is often grouped with lumber (and other construction material) products, and reports sometimes omit ancillary business such as chemical traffic. However, by the 1940s, some sources estimated that 1 in every 15 North American freight car loads were related to the pulp and paper industry.

Although trucks have captured some of this traffic (especially short-haul pulpwood and wood chip loads), railroads remain a key carrier of other raw materials and finished products. As of 2023, railroads moved about 700,000 carloads of pulp and paper products annually. The industry is among the last major users of boxcars: It's estimated that about half of all boxcar loads involve paper and pulp products.

Complex trackwork winding through tight spaces helps make mills visually fascinating places. Duluth & Northeastern served this mill at Cloquet, Minn., using steam power into the early 1960s. Here a 2-8-0 snakes its string of cars (including a coal hopper) around pulpwood loads and Canadian National paper boxcars in 1963. John Gruber

A brief history of paper

Early papyrus (from which "paper" derives its name) dates back several thousand years. This early product was heavier and more resembled a mat compared to modern paper. The first true paper, made in screened forms from fibers obtained from pulped plants, was produced around the first century in China, but the process remained a secret from the rest of the world for several centuries.

Papermaking eventually spread across the Far East, making it to Europe around the 10th century. The process was still slow and laborious, with finished paper products largely the property of governments and the rich. An early landmark was the Gutenburg printing press in 1456, which helped spur demand for paper.

Although paper production increased, the process remained slow and cumbersome. At the time, most paper was produced using fibers obtained from cotton and linen rags, with pulp processed by hand and paper made in screens in sheet-by-sheet fashion.

The first true paper factory in what would become the United States began production in 1690 in Germantown, Pa., although its capacity was a mere 100 pounds of paper per day — all made by hand. Other mills soon appeared, but together they couldn't keep up with demand.

TOP 10 NORTH AMERICAN PAPER COMPANIES, 1970		
Rank	Company	Production (tons)
1	International Paper	4,372,000
2	Georgia-Pacific	2,741,000
3	Crown Paper Corp.	2,665,000
4	St. Regis Paper Co.	2,193,000
5	Weyerhaeuser	2,072,000
6	Kimberly-Clark Corp.	1,716,000
7	Union Camp Corp.	1,440,000
8	Great Northern Paper Inc.	1,405,000
9	Scott Paper Co.	1,333,000
10	Container Corp. of America	1,278,000

TOP 10 NORTH AMERICAN PULP AND PAPER COMPANIES, 2023	
1	International Paper
2	Georgia-Pacific
3	WestRock
4	Packaging Corporation of America
5	Domtar Inc.
6	Graphic Packaging International
7	Billerud AB (Sweden)
8	Sylvamo Corp.
9	Sappi Ltd.
10	Kimberly-Clark Corp.

The traditional method of moving pulpwood logs was floating them down a river or along a lake. The method lasted in some areas into the 1940s. Here a pikeman is keeping logs moving on a sluiceway in Maine in the early 1940s.
Library of Congress

A lot of pulpwood moved by rail through the steam and early diesel eras. The Burlington Northern's Ashland (Wis.) turn is heading out of Superior, Wis., bound for an Ashland mill on the former Great Northern around 1970.
J. David Ingles

It took two breakthroughs to make paper affordable and turn it into a common, widely used product. The first was the mechanical papermaking machine. In the late 1700s, Frenchman Nicholas Luis Robert developed a machine that used a revolving (endless) wire mesh that produced a seamless length of paper. The machine was further developed, improved, and made practical by the Fourdrinier brothers, Henry and Sealy, who patented their machine in England in 1806. The machines that revolutionized the industry carried the brothers' name, and within a few decades most paper mills in Europe and North America were using machine technology.

The second development that made large-scale paper production practical was the ability to obtain fibers from wood, a readily available raw material. The first experiments (a process called "pulping") in the 1840s did this mechanically by grinding wood to capture fibers. A mill in Valleyfield, Quebec was the first to do it on a large scale in North America in 1866. Chemical pulping processes, which dissolve the body of the wood to capture the fibers, increased efficiency and allowed larger-scale operations. Canada's first sulfite mill opened in 1887, and others were soon in operation.

From that point onward, paper machines would become larger and faster, pulping processes would be revised and become more efficient, mills would grow in size, and the industry — with the growing population on the continent — would expand dramatically.

Rapid growth

A major factor in the growth of the paper industry was the need for newsprint. As U.S. population grew, newspapers became increasingly popular. Printing presses — like paper-making machines — were growing in size and capacity. Large cities boasted multiple

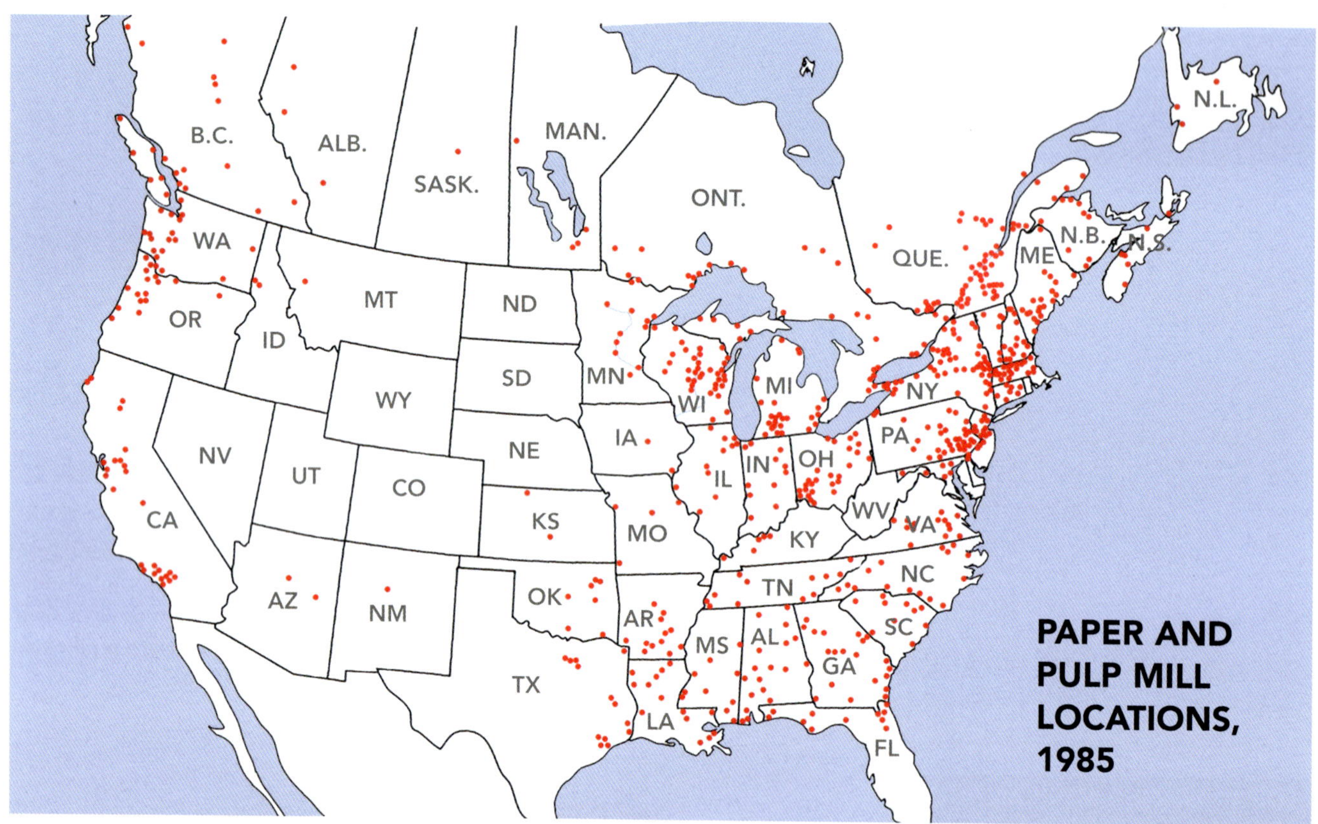

Dots represent U.S. and Canadian paper and pulp mills in operation as of 1985. They are concentrated in four main areas: Northeast, Midwest, South/Southeast, and Northwest. *Firecrown Media illustration*

daily papers, and most small towns and cities had at least weekly or twice-weekly newspapers.

Newspaper circulation in the U.S. increased by 80% from 1870 to 1909, and by another 50% by 1929. American newsprint production likewise grew dramatically, from 100,000 tons in 1869 to 1.1 million tons in 1914.

Into the 1900s, the U.S. produced more paper than Canada, but this would soon change. American paper consumption (and population) was increasing dramatically, but Canada had vastly larger forests to provide raw materials, with lower population to consume finished mill products. The number of Canadian mills (and their paper output) was increasing, Canadian mills were growing larger than their U.S. contemporaries, and American printers (namely newspapers) were importing a significant amount of Canadian paper.

A key at the time was that Canadian newsprint (which had lower production costs, largely from mills' proximity to plentiful wood sources), although cheaper, was subject to an import tariff. This was repealed in 1911 (taking effect in 1913) and greatly increased the amount of Canadian newsprint entering the U.S.

In 1911, Canada had 54 mills; in 1917 there were 83 mills, producing 684,000 tons of newsprint, and by 1930 newsprint production was about 2.9 million tons, compared to 2.1 million tons from U.S. mills (Canada exported all but 5% of its total newsprint production). By the 1920s, Canada was supplying the U.S. with a third of its newsprint, and by the early 1940s, the total was 70%.

Through this period, railroads were responsible for carrying most raw materials in and finished products out. Trucks were small, and roads were still largely unpaved — especially in rural areas where pulpwood was collected and many mills were located. To receive logs, some mills still relied on the traditional method of floating them along waterways, but logs delivered by railcar — boxcars in many cases, together with specialized bulkhead flats — were becoming more common by the 1930s.

TOP PAPER-PRODUCING STATES, 2000

		(MILLIONS OF TONS)
1	Georgia	10.415
2	Alabama	9.536
3	Louisiana	7.437
4	Washington	7.265
5	Wisconsin	7.129
6	Michigan	5.212
7	South Carolina	4.911
8	Maine	4.796
9	Oregon	4.657
10	Virginia	4.638

Finished paper products were shipped by boxcar. This required a vast number of clean cars in good repair, especially for the large rolls of newsprint that comprised the bulk of traffic. Photos of mills through the 1940s show a sea of boxcars, with pulpwood cars and a few tank cars along mill trackage.

Chemicals were largely shipped in barrels or drums in boxcars, although by the 1930s high-pressure tank cars

Truss-rod flatcars with angle-braced bulkheads carry loads into a pulp yard on the Duluth & Northern Minnesota at Knife River, Minn., in 1915. Franklin A. King collection

and specialized acid tank cars became more common. Dry materials such as powdered clay, corn starch, and lime were largely shipped in bags or sacks in boxcars. Covered hoppers would become common for these materials by the 1950s, with slurry tank cars a couple of decades later. See chapters 5 to 8 for details on the freight cars used in the industry.

Regional growth

The number of paper and pulp mills continued growing in the early 1900s, and they became larger, requiring more capital investment for more advanced technology and equipment. As this happened, the industry grew primarily in four regions, all tied to large forests of various types of timber suited to making pulp and paper. The map on page 10 shows this in more detail.

The first area to develop was the Northeast: from northern and central Maine stretching downward through New York and into eastern Pennsylvania and New Jersey, and in Canada along the St. Lawrence River in Quebec, northward into New

Barges and ships also transported paper. Here paper rolls are being transloaded from barges to boxcars by crane on the New York, Ontario & Western at Oswego, N.Y., in 1944. Workers are muscling the rolls into the New York Central steel boxcars with handcarts. General Electric

Brunswick and into Nova Scotia, and westward into several areas in eastern Ontario.

As U.S. population grew and shifted westward, mills began growing in the Midwest. These were built from Ohio and Michigan north- and westward across northern Wisconsin and Minnesota, and in Ontario along the north banks of Lake Superior and into eastern Manitoba.

The early 1900s, especially the period just after World War I, saw a growth in paper mills in the Northwest, stretching from western Oregon and Washington northward into British Columbia, with scattered mills inland and into northern California. Another isolated pocket was farther south, in tree-abundant areas along the Pacific Coast just south of Los Angeles.

The fourth major region to develop was the American South and Southeast, from eastern Texas through Arkansas and Louisiana, eastward to the coast, and northward through the Carolinas into Virginia. Paper mills in this region developed in the 1930s and later as technology evolved to allow efficient processing of the southern pine trees that dominated the region.

The types of paper produced in each region — and the processes used — vary based on the age of the mills and the types of trees used as raw material. In addition, U.S. mills in some areas (primarily the Northeast) imported pulpwood from Canada: 12% of total pulpwood used in the U.S. in 1940 came from Canada.

Modern consolidation and change

Since the 1940s, paper and pulp mills — like many other large industries — have greatly expanded production, but with fewer, larger plants. Mills with older, slower, less-efficient papermaking machines have been shut down or upgraded with newer, faster, more efficient machines and processes. The type of paper produced at many mills has remained the same, with others shifting to different products to reflect changes in the market for specific types of paper. Most mills today are integrated, producing pulp as well as finished products. There are, however, many smaller specialty mills still in operation, making items ranging from adhesive labels to heat-sensitive printing paper.

International pulp and paper production has expanded significantly, especially in South America and Asia, which affected North American production, imports, and exports. The world market for various types of paper fluctuates significantly year to year.

The most notable examples in recent years have been the rise of online shopping and the falling circulation for newspapers and print magazines. This has led to a sharp drop in demand for newsprint and coated magazine papers in the new century. However, demand for corrugated cardboard and other packaging materials for shipping has increased, and demand for tissues and paper towels is also up.

In 1941, there were more than 500 paper companies in the U.S., producing 17.3 million tons of paper. By 2023, annual American production exceeded 60 million tons, but with far fewer mills (about 200) and companies. The top 10 companies listed on page 14 control most of the market; all have multiple mills, many in several coun-

Machines produce paper in a continuous sheet, passing it around dozens of rollers as it progresses from wet to dry. This machine is at the Mississquoi paper mill at Sheldon Springs, Vt., in 1941. Safety guards were a later development. Jack Delano, Library of Congress

This newsprint roll is a product of the Spruce Falls Power & Paper Co., an Ontario company co-owned by the *New York Times* and Kimberly-Clark. Here *Times* employees are moving the 1,700-pound roll from the warehouse to the pressroom in 1942. Marjory Collins, Library of Congress

Modern paper machines can stretch more than 300 feet long and stand 30 feet tall. A worker adjusts a machine at a Willamette mill in Pennsylvania in the 1990s. Jim Hediger

Although trucks have taken many traffic types in the industry, railroads still haul plenty of finished paper products. Here a switcher of Genesee & Wyoming's Buffalo & Pittsburgh subsidiary pulls a cut of boxcars from the Willamette paper mill at DuBois, Pa., in the 1990s. Jim Hediger

U.S. PAPER PRODUCTION BY TYPE, 2023	
TYPE	TONS
Packaging and paperboard	50,721,000
Tissue/sanitary/household	7,763,000
Uncoated graphic/printing/writing	4,601,000
Other/Misc.	1,747,000
Coated graphic/printing/writing	1,582,000
Other graphic paper	625,000
Newsprint	325,000

tries. All told, 38% of harvested trees in the U.S. (about 228 million tons per year) are used to make paper products.

The Canadian paper industry suffered huge downturns and mill closings from the late 1990s into the 2000s as newsprint demand shrank. Canadian newsprint production peaked at 9.3 million tons in 1994, but dropped to 4.6 million tons in 2010 and 1.8 million tons by 2021.

In spite of that, Canada is still a significant producer of paper — 9.9 million tons in 2023 — ranking 10th in world production. Canadian mills have shifted some production to packaging paper, and the country is a world leader in kraft pulp exports and is growing in production of "fine paper." Canada exports about two-thirds of its paper products, with companies in the U.S. taking about three-quarters of those exports.

Rail transport

The growth of interstate highways and other improved roads, along with increasing truck and trailer sizes, has led to trucks capturing a greater share of mill-related traffic. This is especially true for inbound logs and chips, with many mills receiving 100% of their wood raw material by truck. Railroads have retained some of this traffic

Modern paper mills are huge operations, covering several acres. This integrated mill is the combined Alabama River Pulp Co. and Claiborne Mill in Claiborne, Ala. The photo shows, from left, cooling towers, chip piles and conveyors, digesters, and process buildings and storage tanks. Carol M. Highsmith, Library of Congress

(mainly chips) in some regions.

Chemicals and many additives (such as kaolin clay slurry and titanium dioxide slurry) are moved by rail in significant amounts to mills, as they lend themselves to the efficiency of moving by tank car.

And although trucks now deliver a higher percentage of finished paper products, railroads still haul a great deal of it (especially large rolls) in boxcars to distribution centers throughout the country, with final delivery to customers often by truck.

ENVIRONMENTAL ISSUES AND CHANGE

The paper industry unfortunately does not have a good history of caring for the environment. Through the mid-1900s, mills were often large sources of pollution, with untreated chemicals and wastewater released directly into rivers and lakes, large amounts of air pollution including coal smoke and sulfur dioxide, and ground contamination from various byproducts. Forests were often cut without regard to future regrowth.

This has largely changed since the 1960s, with tougher government rules and standards. Mills now feature on-site wastewater treatment plants. Processes are more efficient, using less energy and cleaner-burning fuels, with advanced emissions controls. Waste products can often be burned as fuel. Fewer hazardous chemicals are used: For example, the use of elemental chlorine for bleaching has largely been replaced by chlorine dioxide and other methods. Paper recycling has become a major source of pulp, saving energy and timber. Foresting has become a science, with timber areas managed to ensure that the land can be reused and trees regrown.

CHAPTER TWO

HOW PAPER IS MADE

Most papermaking processes take place out of sight, within the various buildings of a mill. The billowing clouds and lots of activity (rail, vehicle, and person) on the outside are signs that mill operations are progressing. At modern mills, the emissions from stacks and vents is mainly steam, but early mills unfortunately emitted large quantities of smoke and sulfur dioxide among other pollutants. This is a Menasha, Wis., mill in 1998. Jim Hediger

Before we look at paper mills and their ties to railroads, it's important to understand the basics of papermaking itself. We'll explain how pulp is made and processed, how it's used to make various types of paper, and see what raw materials go into the process. We'll also look at the machines and processes involved and how they've evolved.

Wood is mechanically ground into pulp at the Mississquoi Corp. mill in Sheldon Springs, Vt., in 1941. In pre-OSHA days, many mill jobs were hot, noisy, and dangerous.
Jack Delano, Library of Congress

A look inside the digester building at the Champion mill in Houston, Texas, shows the tall vessels used for "cooking" the pulp. The view is from 1943.
John Vachon, Library of Congress

Another view from the Mississquoi mill in 1941 shows a worker stirring pulp in a vat. Workers of the era were exposed to hazardous chemicals, as well as dangers from heat. Jack Delano, Library of Congress

What is paper?

Paper is a sheet material made from cellulose fibers, which typically come from wood but sometimes from cotton or other plants. We'll focus on paper made from wood, which since the mid-1800s has been the primary raw material for paper products.

The key ingredient in paper is the fibers, tiny hollow tubes with closed ends that measure about 1mm to 3mm in length. The papermaking process involves capturing the fibers by mechanical or chemical means, treating them, and combining them with fillers and binders to form a smooth sheet material. Coniferous (soft) woods generally have the longest fibers — resulting in stronger paper — and are the primary base for most types of paper.

What the industry considers "paper" comprises a wide variety of materials and finished products. Along with writing paper and newsprint, other products produced by paper mills include tissue papers (napkins, facial tissues, paper towels, and hygiene products), cardboard (single-ply material

The heart of any paper mill is the paper machine. Modern machines, like this one at the Claiborne, Ala., mill, can stretch 300 feet long and stand three stories tall. The building housing the machine is usually the largest and longest in the complex. Carol M. Highsmith, Library of Congress

of many weights, as well as corrugated material for packaging), coated paper (beverage and food cartons, paper cups, waxed paper), adhesive-backed paper (labels and tape), heat-transfer paper (printing, graphics, point-of-sale receipts), molded pulp packaging (egg cartons, beverage holders, and many types of custom-fit product packaging), food-wrapping paper, filter paper, and any number of colored and textured products from construction and crepe paper to "fine paper" — high-quality coated or uncoated writing and graphic card and paper products.

Pulp destined for storage or shipping to other mills is pressed, dried, and cut into sheets or rolls, left. Like finished paper, it travels in boxcars, right; unlike paper rolls, it leaves a mess behind. This boxcar will have to be cleaned before carrying another load. Two photos: Jim Hediger

Stacks of kraft pulp have been unloaded from boxcars onto a dock at the Southland Paper Co. mill in Lufkin, Texas, in 1943. The pulp, delivered from another mill, will be added to the groundwood pulp produced at Southland to make newsprint. John Vachon, Library of Congress

By the late 1800s the process of making paper had become mechanized, and by the 1890s, mills were turning out products in high volumes and were developing better, more efficient ways of processing wood.

The papermaking process is divided into two distinct steps or processes: making pulp and making paper. There are mills that only make pulp (pulp mills), mills that only make paper (finishing, converter, or specialty mills), and mills that do both — called "integrated mills." Most modern mills are integrated. "Market pulp" is the term for pulp produced at one location and sold to mills at other locations.

To obtain the cellulose fibers, they must be separated from the surrounding lignin, which forms much of the body of the wood structure and binds it all together. Getting the pulp, or fibers, is done using one of two basic

Liquid stock — the thinned mixture of pulp and fillers — starts its journey on the moving screen at the wet end of the paper machine at the Southland mill. John Vachon, Library of Congress

processes — mechanical or chemical. Each of these has multiple variations, some of which are combined with pressure and high temperature.

The first step (for all but the groundwood method) is to grind the wood into small, uniformly sized pieces: under an inch long and no more than 3⁄16" thick. (Chapter 3 provides more details on this process.)

Mechanical pulping

There are a couple of variations in the mechanical process. For the oldest method, the groundwood process, a short log ("bolt") of wood is ground against a rotating wet stone. Water carries the material from the stone; it is then screened to separate the fibers and remove impurities. The water is then removed, leaving behind the pulp.

A more advanced variation is shredding wood chips between rotating steel discs in a vessel called a refiner, producing "refiner mechanical pulp" (RMP). The resulting pulp is stronger with less fiber damage than groundwood pulp.

A further refinement is thermomechanical pulping, where the wood chips are heated with steam under pressure (or chemically pretreated) prior to grinding. This takes more energy, but again improves the quality of the recovered fibers.

Advantages of mechanical pulping are that it's less expensive than chemical processes, avoids most dangerous chemicals, recovers a high percentage of fibers (close to 90%), and results in paper that takes ink well.

However, mechanical pulp is lower quality than chemical pulp, as the fibers are often damaged in the pulping process and some lignin remains in the resulting pulp — the resulting paper tends to yellow over time. The process also requires more energy than chemical pulping.

Mechanical pulp is generally used for low-quality (often disposable) paper and board, such as newsprint, low-grade book paper, and packaging. It's often blended with chemical pulp to produce intermediate-grade paper. Traditional newsprint, for example, typically included 75% groundwood and 25% chemical pulp.

A worker checks the size of a roll of paper at the dry end of a paper machine. Jim Hediger

In 1920, U.S. mills produced 1.57 million tons of mechanical pulp, with Canadian mills adding 846,000 tons. Although chemical pulp is far more common today, there's still a market for mechanical pulp, with U.S. mill capacity near 300,000 tons annually.

Chemical pulping

As the name implies, chemical pulping uses various compounds to dissolve the non-fiber materials in wood, leaving just the fibers (pulp). The chief advantage of chemical processes is that the resulting pulp is high quality, resulting in strong paper that can be easily bleached. Disadvantages are that it's a more expensive process, it recovers only about half of the wood fibers (meaning much more raw materials are needed), and presents many hazards because the chemicals involved.

There are several types of chemical pulping, and although the steps involved are largely the same, the specific chemicals involved differ. You don't need a chemical engineer's knowledge of the processes to model the operations effectively, but having a basic understanding of the methods and how they vary will help you picture what's going on behind the modeled walls of your paper mill buildings.

Here are brief summaries of the major chemical pulping methods:

Sulfite process: In the early 1880s, experiments showed that by cooking wood chips in a sulfur dioxide solution in water, with lime added, dissolved the non-fibrous portions of the wood. Further experiments led to large-scale operations, and the sulfite process was first used in North American mills in the late 1800s. Sulfite remained the dominant process into the 1930s. Although some mills still use the process, no new sulfite mills have been built since the 1960s.

Its main advantage is that it results in a stable, easily bleached pulp that can be turned into high-quality paper. However, the sulfite process is expensive (largely due to the chemicals and processes involved) and it is not a clean one: sulfur dioxide emissions are a major problem for both air and water. Many of the chemicals involved are hazardous and present inhalation and skin exposure hazards to workers.

Soda process: The oldest chemical process uses sodium hydroxide (better known as caustic soda) with slaked lime (obtained when limestone is burned in a kiln) at high temperatures and pressure to break down the lignin and separate the fibers. It was invented in the United Kingdom in the early 1850s and was being used in North American mills by the 1860s. It was a dominant method in the northeastern U.S. into the early 1900s.

The resulting pulp isn't as strong as sulfite pulp, and the fiber yield is low compared to other methods. Soda pulp waste (high in alkali) presents many environmental problems. The method is still used in some mills, mainly for processing hardwoods and non-wood raw materials, but most soda mills shifted to the kraft/sulfate process by the mid-1900s.

Sulfate/kraft process: What is commonly called the "kraft pulp" process is a modification of the soda process ("kraft" means strength in

The finished paper emerges from the dry end of the machine and is rolled onto a reel drum. When it is full, a new spool is lowered into place while the old reel is removed — all while the machine is running. This is the Southland mill in 1943.
John Vachon, Library of Congress

Finished, trimmed paper rolls are wrapped, labeled, and stored for shipment. The Southland mill in 1943 used a "jitney" lift to move these newsprint rolls from the winding department to the warehouse and eventually to the dock for shipping.
John Vachon, Library of Congress

German). It was introduced in 1880s and began appearing at large mills around 1910. It still uses caustic soda, but with sodium sulfide. The process is faster than the soda process, captures more fibers, and results in a stronger paper. Another advantage is that many chemicals can be recovered instead of discharged as waste.

A disadvantage is that the resulting pulp has a dark brown color, so requires bleaching for many final products. The process still results in sulfur dioxide emissions that can present environmental challenges.

The kraft process became popular in North America after World War I, especially for the growing number of new mills being built in the southeast U.S., where the process works especially well with southern pines (which have a great deal of resin in the wood). About 75% of modern pulp production in the U.S. uses the kraft process.

How pulping is done

"Cooking" — the process of pulping in any of the chemical processes — takes place in multiple vertical towers or tanks within a building. The process starts in a large vessel called a digester. The digester is steel, but lined to protect against the acids involved. Digester size varies by era and type of mill, but by the 1930s, a 15- to 35-ton capacity was common. A 23-ton digester of the period measured about 17 feet in diameter and 70 feet tall (about 50,000 gallons); modern digesters are this size or slightly larger.

The chemicals required for each process are stored nearby in large tanks. Their size and style will vary by the era, mill capacity, and specific process being used.

The digester is filled with wood chips and the acid mix is then pumped in. Steam is introduced to bring up the temperature. In direct cooking ("quick cooking"), the steam is introduced directly into the digester, bringing the temperature to around 280 to 300 degrees (F). With indirect cooking, steam passes through coils inside the digester, raising the temp to 250-275 degrees. The pressure also rises, to about 70-80 psi.

The cooking time for a batch ("charge") varies by process and the size of the digester — about 2 to 4 hours for kraft and up to 10 hours with the sulfite process. Many modern mills have continuous-charge capabilities instead of processing single batches.

When the charge is complete, waste from the process (lignin, wood resin, spent chemicals) is drained. This toxic liquid is called "black liquor." It goes to a recovery tank "evaporator" which concentrates the material. Some caustic soda and other chemicals (alcohols, turpentine) can often be reclaimed, again, depending upon the process; the remainder is often burned as fuel.

In a kraft mill, one recovery step includes running a division of the waste products through a rotary lime kiln. The process results in reburned lime that is then recycled in the cooking process (called "recausticizing").

The pulp itself goes through multiple washes and coarse and fine screenings under agitation ("beating") to clean it and separate any remaining

In the winding department, the full rolls of paper from the machine are unwound, trimmed to the sizes needed by the customer, and rewound into rolls of the needed lengths. This is at the Willamette mill in DuBois, Pa., in the 1990s. Jim Hediger

waste material (wood slivers, uncooked chips) from the wood fibers. The water captured from the washing and later pressing processes ("white water") is then further filtered and processed to recapture any fibers that remain. The initial water removal is called dewatering, slushing, or deckering.

The resulting pulp is now in thick liquid form. If it's to be used at the producing mill in short term, it will be stored in this form in tanks with internal agitators.

If pulp is to be stored long term or shipped, it must be further dried by extracting the water. The pulp goes through a wet press to remove water in an endless belt system. The sheets may also go through a hydraulic press to remove even more moisture (done to save weight for shipping) or a roller-style drying machine using steam to heat and evaporate the water.

The pulp is then rolled, cut into sheets, folded, or lapped into a bundle ("lapping"). Soda pulp is always shipped in rolls; groundwood pulp in laps. Sulphite and kraft pulp can be stored and shipped either way.

When pulp is shipped by rail, boxcars should be clean, preferably lined with kraft paper or similar material on the walls. Rolls are packed on end, with sheets or additional rolls placed on top. Pulp is lighter than finished paper, so a boxcar can be packed tightly.

Bleaching pulp

Pulp is often bleached to make it brighter and whiter, depending on its intended purpose. A common early bleaching agent was "bleaching powder" (chlorinated lime), made by absorbing chlorine gas with nearly dry calcium hydrate (slaked lime). In the steam era, this would typically be delivered to mills in steel drums weighing 750 pounds.

By the 1930s it became more common to use liquid (elemental) chlorine for bleaching, mixed with milk of lime (a white liquid — calcium hydroxide suspended in water). The paper industry eventually became the largest consumer of chlorine in North America.

Elemental chlorine is a hazardous material that presents many challenges in handling. It can result in contaminated water and air, and the bleaching process with chlorine can produce dioxins as a waste byproduct. It was phased out of use by U.S. mills in 2001 by EPA regulation, and even before then it was being replaced by chlorine dioxide — which results in fewer toxic waste byproducts — at many mills. Hydrogen peroxide is another chemical used for bleaching and other purposes at mills.

Some modern mills are TCF ("totally chlorine free") or PCF ("processed chlorine free"), using oxygen-based compounds instead of chlorine for bleaching. Others use ozone as a bleach but still use chlorine dioxide in some steps.

For a pulp mill, this is where the steps end. The resulting pulp will be shipped to finishing mills or integrated mills. At an integrated mill, the process will continue; at a finishing mill, the process starts with receiving pulp from a pulp mill.

CHEMICALS AND ADDITIVES USED IN PAPERMAKING

Many of the chemicals used in papermaking are quite hazardous and toxic, and the working environment in many mills — especially in the years prior to OSHA and modern safety regulations — presented many dangers. A rather matter-of-fact note in a papermaking textbook from the late 1920s had this warning: "Men have been known to stumble and fall into a tank of caustic soda — nothing was recovered but a few coins and teeth. Be careful!"

Below is a list of the most common chemicals and materials used in the papermaking process, along with their common purpose. Specific additives vary widely by process and era (not all are included):

Aluminum sulfate: Binding agent
Calcium carbonate (chalk): Filler; increases opacity and strength
Caustic soda (sodium hydroxide): dissolves lignin in wood, separating fibers
Chlorine: Bleaching agent; also used to treat wastewater
Dolomite (calcium magnesium carbonate): Filler, coating
Hydrochloric acid: Wastewater treatment; acid processes
Hydrogen peroxide: Bleaching agent
Kaolin clay (and Bentonite clay): Filler; increases opacity and smoothness
Limestone or lime slurry: Used in acid-making process
Rosin (cationic rosin): pulp-sizing agent, makes paper water resistant
Sodium carbonate (soda ash): Controls pH levels during pulping
Sodium sulfide: Bleaching agent
Sodium chlorate: Used with acid to make chlorine dioxide for bleaching
Starch: Paper coating and binder
Titanium dioxide (Titania): Filler and coating; increases opacity and brightness

** See chapter 8 for details on railcar transport of these materials*

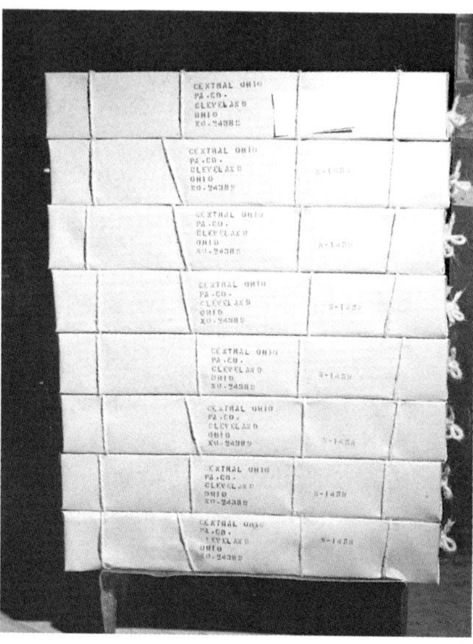

Paper and cardboard are sometimes stored and shipped flat, based on the needs of customers. Here cardboard is trimmed at stacked at the Mississquoi mill in 1941, left. It is then wrapped and labeled, above, before shipping. Jack Delano, Library of Congress

Stock

The pulp is blended in a tank with other ingredients to create "stock," which goes into a paper machine to create the final paper product. Multiple types of pulp (included recycled fiber) are often combined to obtain different paper characteristics, so even an integrated mill may receive shipments of market pulp from other mills.

Kaolin clay (which makes paper smooth and increases opacity) is the most common filler; bentonite clay is sometimes used, which also acts to bind the fibers better and allows better drainage, providing a stronger product. Other common additives are titanium dioxide and calcium carbonate, both of which increase brightness and make paper glossy. Starch or another resin is applied during the process as a binder.

The stock mix is very thin — about 99.5% water — so it will flow freely. It is then ready for the paper machine.

Paper machines

Machines that produce a continuous output sheet of paper have historically been of two designs. Fourdrinier machines have a moving screen belt onto which the stock is sprayed at the headbox (at the "wet end" of the machine), with an even, thin coat of stock applied to the screen. As the belt moves, water is continually removed by a combination of gravity, pressure, heat, and suction. The now-formed film sheet then separates from the screen and passes around a series of presses and steam-heated cylinders (up to 100 cylinders in large machines). This forms and dries the paper as it moves, and it eventually emerges at the "dry end" of the machine.

Later cylinder-style machines have cylinders covered with screen mesh instead of a moving belt. The cylinder picks up a film of the stock mix as it rotates through a vat. The film separates and passes around a further series of cylinders, including felted-covered cylinders, being dried along the way, until it emerges at the dry end.

Late in the process the formed paper is "calendered," passing through large rollers that press it to the desired thickness and smoothness; additional coatings are added as required.

As the finished paper emerges from the dry end, it's taken up on a spool called a reel drum, where it's wound into a roll. When the roll reaches the proper size, a new spool is lowered into place and the full roll removed. Because paper machines run continuously, this is done while the paper is moving.

Once each roll is removed from the machine, it is cut to its final trim width in the "winder" department. The roll is unwound from its spool, passes through sharp cutters called "slitters" to its desired width, and the newly cut paper is rewound into a roll of the desired size needed by the customer. The roll is then wrapped to protect it, labeled, and stored until it's ready for shipping.

Paper can also be sheeted (cut into sheets of specific sizes) depending upon customers' needs. It can also be fully cut to finished size and packaged; paper is often shipped to another facility for this. As paper is rolled and cut to final size, any trimmings and scrap are taken back and recycled directly to the pulping department.

This is a greatly simplified explanation of an extremely complex machine, but it provides an idea of the processes involved.

Paper machines are rated by size (the width of the finished sheet) and speed in feet per minute (fpm), as well as their annual capacity to produce paper (in tons). A typical machine of the late 1800s had a speed of about 100 fpm with a 100"-wide roll; by the early 1900s this had grown to 500 fpm at 160". Even in the 1940s, machines were huge. A new Fourdrinier machine of that period could weigh 1,500 tons, stand two stories tall and stretch more than 200 feet in length. A large modern machine stands three stories tall and can be 300 feet or longer.

Some modern machines have speeds that top 6,000 fpm with a trim width of 240", and can produce 300,000 or more tons of paper annually. Because of the investments involved, these machines must run continuously — other than routine maintenance — to make it worth the cost.

Turn the page and we'll look at how a paper mill accomplishes all of these operations.

At the Southland plant, a worker uses a lift truck (jitney) to load rolls of newsprint into a boxcar in 1943. The car is a 40-foot single-sheathed design (see more on paper cars in Chapter 5). John Vachon, Library of Congress

CHAPTER THREE

PAPER MILLS AND OPERATIONS

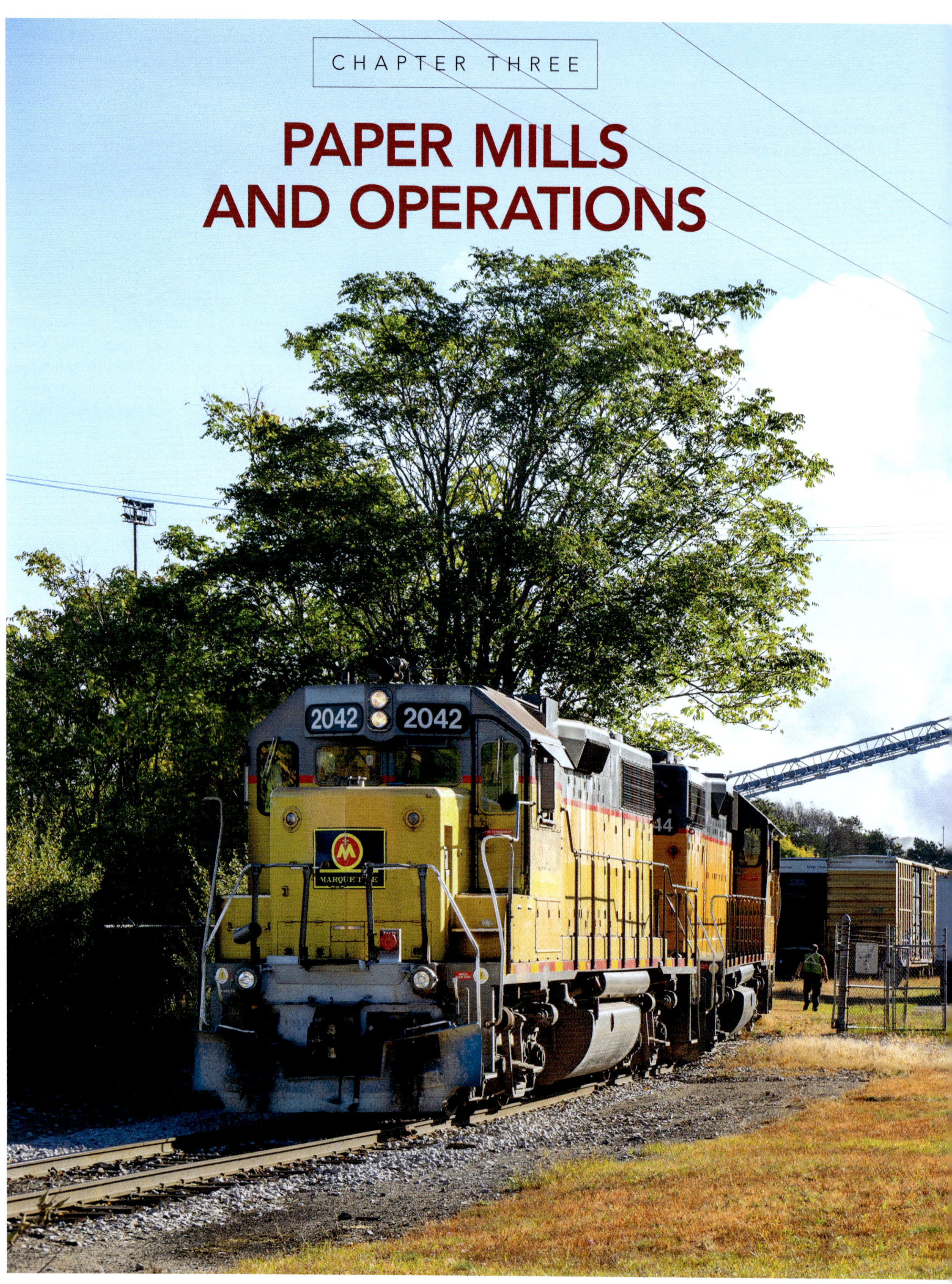

A paper mill is a factory complex where all of the processes described in Chapter 2 take place. The scope and size of mills increased dramatically from the late 1800s into the early 1900s. Modern mills are huge, covering several acres, with multiple buildings and extensive railroad trackage throughout the property.

Marquette Rail GP38-2 No. 2042 switches the Packaging Corporation of America paper mill at Filer City, Mich., in October 2024. A crewman is walking through the gate toward the mill's yard, which holds strings of boxcars at left. The wood chip pile at right is steaming on this cold day, while the digester building stands in the background. Steve Smedley

Mills fall into three basic categories based on what they produce. A pulp mill, as the name implies, only makes pulp, shipping the final product ("market pulp") to other mills. A mill that makes paper exclusively from pulp obtained from other mills is called a finishing, converter, or specialty mill. And a mill that both produces pulp and processes it into paper is an integrated mill — most modern mills are integrated.

Integrated mills are typically larger, usually producing a single type (or limited types) of paper. Non-integrated mills can be smaller, and are more likely to produce multiple types of products or shift from type to type as the market changes.

Paper mills of all types lend themselves to modeling, with their fascinating mix of structures, tanks, bins, wood storage piles, and other equipment. Important for modelers is the extensive trackwork at mills and multiple types of freight cars that serve the industry. A mill can be a prominent industry

The cars on the foreground track are open-top cars (covered by snow) for carrying pulp logs and sawdust within the paper mill at Berlin, N.H., in 1940. The dozens of boxcars on the rear tracks are loaded. Many have had material tacked vertically on the door edges to better seal them and protect the paper loads. Marion Post Wolcott, Library of Congress

Paper mills are large, sprawling complexes, and their need for large supplies of water means they're located on rivers or lakes. This 1990s view shows Appleton Papers at Kaukauna, Wis., along the Fox River. The digester complex and power plant are at left, with the long papermaking building at right. Jim Hediger

WHAT'S A CORD OF WOOD?

As with other timber, pulpwood logs are generally measured and sold by the cord instead of by the pound or ton, because the weight of various types of wood varies so much. A cord is defined as a tightly stacked pile measuring 4 x 4 x 8 feet (128 cubic feet).

Log weight depends on whether it is softwood or hardwood (and upon the specific species), and whether it is green (recently cut, with moisture content near 100%) or dry. Hardwood is heavier than soft. As an example of the extreme weight variations, a cord of green hardwood can weigh around 5,000 pounds, while a cord of dry softwood might weigh just 2,000 pounds.

Pulpwood logs are unloaded from boxcars, rack cars, and storage piles at the Southland paper mill in Lufkin, Texas, in 1943. The chain conveyor (left) takes the logs to the debarker. Mechanical unloaders (right) greatly sped the process compared to loading and unloading cars by hand. Two photos: John Vachon, Library of Congress

Pulpwood logs emerge from the barking machine, a rotating drum that tumbles logs to remove bark. Logs with remaining bark are placed on a conveyor and pass through the machine a second time. John Vachon, Library of Congress

on a large layout, and can even be the entire focus of a smaller layout.

Although all paper mills share many similar processes and details, it's important to understand that no two mills are alike. Their layout and construction differ, and they vary in size, by the pulping process (mechanical, soda, sulfite, kraft), and by age. A 1940s Canadian mill producing newsprint will appear quite a bit different than a 1980s mill in the southern U.S. making tissue paper.

This chapter, therefore (and the book as a whole) has to be rather general in many descriptions. The many detail variations work to the favor of modelers, as it enables us to customize the appearance to match specific prototypes. If you're modeling a specific mill, try to obtain photos if possible.

We'll look at typical mill locations, the various structures, stockpiles, and details (and how they're all laid out), and how the processes in Chapter 2 are carried out among the mill buildings.

Modern mills are more likely to handle pulp as tree-length logs. This is the Alabama River Pulp Co., at Claiborne, Ala., in 2010. Carol M. Highsmith, Library of Congress

We'll also look at typical track layouts and see how rail operations mesh with the mill complex and operations.

Basic considerations

The first consideration is location. Pulp and integrated mills are located near a primary source of wood. As Chapter 1 showed, this means primarily the U.S. Northeast, South, and West, plus eastern and western Canada.

Mills are almost always located on a river or body of water, as a plentiful source is vital. A modern mill uses from 4,000 to 12,000 gallons of water for every ton of bleached pulp produced, per the U.S. Department of Energy, making paper mills North America's largest industrial users of water per ton of product produced.

Historically, many mills (especially in the Northeast) also used water for power. This could be in the form of hydroelectric power produced at dams at or near mill sites, or by using waterways diverted through the mill to

WOOD CHIP BASICS

All wood chips are not equal. The chips that a mill processes itself from roundwood after debarking offer the best control of quality and size, and are the preferred type of chip. Wood chips captured at sawmills and other wood processors as a byproduct of making lumber and wood products are shipped to paper mills as "residual chips." Although they are screened and cleaned, they can still contain a high percentage of bark, sawdust, odd-shaped (or too-large) chips, and waste material.

Entire trees chipped on site where they're harvested are called "whole tree chips." These chips are also subject to contamination from bark and dirt, so must be cleaned and screened. Their chip size can also vary excessively.

Sawdust includes fine granules, slivers, and strands smaller than standard chip size, all of which must be separated from chips before pulping. And although sawdust can often be processed by itself, the resulting fibers are often short and weak. Some sawdust is too fine to use as pulp; it's often burned as fuel.

For calculating shipping rates in railcars and trucks, chips are sold by volume in "units" — one unit is 190 cubic feet. Along with capacity in cubic feet, modern chip cars are often stenciled with their capacity in units.

Twin timber cranes unload railcars (left) and a log truck (middle) in the wood yard of the Sappi paper mill in Cloquet, Minn., in March 2024. Steve Smedley

Wood chip piles are usually fed by overhead conveyors. Multiple piles are used for different wood types. The paved surface helps limit contamination of the chips. Jim Hediger

power equipment (called a "mill run").

Rail service is vital for both bringing in raw materials as well as shipping finished products. This means mills were either built along active rail lines, or branch lines were laid from a nearby main line to serve the mill. Shortline railroads were sometimes built specifically to serve mills, and in many cases these railroads were owned or controlled by the same company that owned the mill. By the 1950s and later, road and highway access also became crucial.

Mills were (and still are) often located in small towns and rural areas (where a town often later developed). In many cases, mills are the primary employer in their town or area — the "factory town" might be largely owned and controlled by the mill, in the same manner as Appalachian coal mines and their factory towns. Mills were often built near other mills, either in the same town or a neighboring town.

By the 1900s, brick construction was typical for paper mill structures. This continued into the 1940s and 1950s in many areas. From that point, steel siding and prefabricated steel buildings became common, as did concrete block. Prefabricated and poured concrete is favored for many modern industrial buildings.

Many older mills display a mix of construction styles, showing where buildings were upgraded and new structures and additions were built over the years. An example might be a new paper-making machine in a long steel prefab structure, with a nearby powerhouse still in traditional brick.

The overall layout of buildings tends to follow the flow of production, from incoming products through the pulp-making process and papermaking to warehousing. However, there are as many variations as there are mills. Available space often dictates this. For example, a long, narrow area between railroad tracks and a river dictates the layout at a rural mill, compared to another mill in a town, where a square or rectangular footprint follows city blocks and streets.

Let's take a look at the key areas of a paper mill, starting with arrival of inbound raw materials. Many of the processes described in Chapter 2 are hidden from view, done inside buildings, so we'll concentrate on the details and building features visible from outside, which will be the keys to modeling.

Wood handling

How logs and wood chips arrive at a mill largely depends upon the era, region, and the distance required for their transport. Modern mills receive wood in the form of either logs or chips, but into the 1940s, all pulpwood arrived as cut logs ("roundwood"), usually called "bolts." Mills began using chips in the 1940s, and their use

A Duluth & Northeastern 2-8-0 shoves a pair of pulpwood gons past storage piles at Northwest Paper's wood yard in Cloquet, Minn., in 1962. John Gruber

increased over the years, amounting to about half of total pulp requirements in the 2020s.

Through the steam era, mills received most pulpwood by rail or water. By the 1950s and later, as roads and highways improved and trucks became larger, faster, and more powerful, trucks began bringing more and more pulpwood directly to mills.

Today, many mills receive logs and chips exclusively by truck; others use trucks for distances under 75-100 miles, with railroads for longer hauls (details on the railcars involved can be found in chapters 6 and 7). It all comes down to economics: If trucks can do it cheaper than railroads, they will get the contracts for the service.

Mills keep a two- or three-month supply of pulpwood and/or wood chips on hand. This ensures continued production in case of supply issues such as transportation, labor issues, or bad weather. Northern mills may increase their stockpiles in the fall to combat decreased pulpwood production in winter.

Wood piles are rotated — that is, wood is used on a first-in, first-processed basis, as wood that's stored too long will degrade and is subject to rotting. This is not a problem for dry wood (below 20% moisture) or saturated wood (about 60% or above). For this reason, and to keep down the risk of fire — which can be catastrophic — wood storage piles are sprayed with water on a regular basis.

AMOUNT OF WOOD NEEDED

The amount of incoming wood required by a mill depends upon its size. A modern mill can process 1 to 2 million tons of chips or bolts per year. You can do the math and see that a million tons is the equivalent of 37 100-ton cars daily; keep in mind, though, that many mills receive much of this by truck, and smaller and older mills require significantly less pulpwood.

A very rough way to estimate wood usage is that 1.5 cords of wood (about 2-4 tons) will produce about 1.5 tons of pulp, which will produce about 1 ton of paper. If you know the annual capacity of a given mill, you can do the math backward to see how much incoming wood is required for its operation.

As an example, a late-steam-era mill that produces 250 tons of paper per day will use about 375 tons of pulp; this requires about 375 cords of wood, or about 1,100 tons, so about 22 50-ton carloads of pulpwood or chips.

Pulpwood delivery and storage

Pulpwood comprises a variety of species. Soft coniferous woods (pine and fir) are most common, but hardwood is used as well. The wood destined for paper mills is generally not desirable for cut lumber products: trees that are bent or aren't large enough to produce sufficient-size boards. Chapter 4 provides an outline of how trees are cut and shipped to mills.

From the 1800s and into the 1900s, mills often received logs that were floated down a river or formed into rafts and moved along a lake. These were typically long (8 feet or longer), cut at lumber camps near the waterway. This was still done in many areas, especially in the Northeast, into the 1940s and later. Ships and barges could also deliver wood.

By the early 1900s, it became more common to deliver wood by rail, especially as lumbering areas moved inland from waterways. Initially these bolts were loaded into boxcars (called "car wood") in 2- to 4-foot lengths. Gondolas and specialized pulpwood flatcars became more common by the 1930s; these bolts were 4 or 5 feet long, and some mills preferred an 8-foot length.

Since the 1990s, the standard for a pulpwood log has been an 8 foot (specifically 100", or 8'-4") length, and

Chip cars are switched into rotary dumpers one by one, as this Northern Pacific Thrall-built gondola in 1966. The chips are dumped into a pit, then conveyed to storage piles. Thrall

Gondola-style chip cars have doors on one or both ends, allowing end dumping. Here a Burlington Northern FMC-built car is dumped at a Pacific Northwest mill in the early 1970s. The mesh cover has been tied off above the door. Burlington Northern

Most chips today are delivered by truck. Lift dumps are common; some mills use pneumatic unloading. Carol M. Highsmith, Library of Congress

some mills now take tree-length wood. It all depends upon the preferences of individual mills. Another typical specification is that logs be a minimum of 3" or 4" in diameter at the small end. Pulpwood is usually measured (and bought and sold) in cords (see "What's a cord of wood?" on page 29).

Cars are unloaded, with the bolts dropped on a chain or belt conveyor. Unloading cars by hand (the only option for boxcars) was extremely labor intensive — the Bangor & Aroostook estimated it took about 2.5 man-hours to unload an average car. The inbound bolts are, if needed, cut to smaller sizes, then the bark is removed prior to stacking in storage piles.

The move to pulpwood rack cars in the 1930s coincided with mills moving to mechanical handling, using claw-style loaders on overhead traveling cranes or mobile cranes or tractors. The conveyor, grabbing multiple bolts at once, takes them either to the slasher — a cutter with multiple circular saws that automatically cuts logs to their desired length — or directly to the debarker.

Wood bark has very little fiber value and can contaminate paper, so it needs to be removed. This is sometimes done in the field, but if it hasn't been done, it is removed at the mill in a process called "barking," "debarking," or "rossing." The machines that do this have a variety of designs, but usually have a long barrel- or tube-shaped vessel called a barking drum. As the logs tumble against each other, the bark is peeled off and separated. If the bark is wet, it goes through a press, and is then either burned on site as fuel or stored and sold (as landscaping or "hog fuel").

The debarked wood is then stored until needed. Bolts can be stacked in rows or dumped in large loose piles, carried by a conveyor called a stacker. The stacker piles the wood, then moves backward to continue the pile when it reaches the desired height. Stacks can range from 50 to 125 feet in height and can occupy several acres. Wood is sorted and stored by species and type until needed.

The ground surface upon which wood is stored must be clean and drain

Debarked logs are conveyed from outdoor storage piles (right) to the grinding room (below) at the Southland mill. The mill produces groundwood pulp; at other mills, the process is similar, but the logs would go to a chipper. Two photos: John Vachon, Library of Congress

Tank cars are unloaded at this Wisconsin mill in a two-track building. Four cars wait outside on a 1990s winter day as a Wisconsin Central local switches boxcars in the background. Jim Hediger

The tank car unloading area at at Willamette Paper in Johnsonburg, Pa., is partially covered. The area includes a concrete containment dike along the tracks, plus hose and pipe connections. The white tank car contains caustic soda (sodium hydroxide). Jim Hediger

A pair of tank cars await unloading at the Crown Vantage mill in Parchment, Mich., while boxcars are parked on a neighboring track. The scene is from the 1990s; the mill closed in 2000. Jim Hediger

well. Cinders were common through the steam era, with gravel over crushed rock since then. Since mills generally use wood in first-in, first-out order, a pile will be reduced to the ground before restocking (progressing along an area) to make sure old wood isn't mixed with new.

One or more spur tracks is usually devoted to log unloading, with loaded cars regularly spotted and empties pulled away. A conveyor pit or channel will run alongside the siding.

Wood storage areas will also have space for truck unloading. This will be more extensive for modern mills, as trucks have gradually claimed more and more of this traffic since the 1950s (and it's 100% by truck for many modern mills).

Wood chip unloading and storage

Mills began receiving wood chips in the 1940s, starting with lumber mills that ground waste material that otherwise would have been burned. Chip use has since grown steadily. Chip use is largely based upon region, with mills in the West more likely to use chips. In the western U.S., 20% of pulp came in the form of chips in 1947; this was 60% by 1960 and 80% by the 2020s. In the East and South in the 2000s only about 20% of inbound wood was in the form of chips.

In Canada, residual chips from sawmills was initially just 2% of raw fiber supplied to mills; by 1990 this had grown to 55% (largely reflecting the integration between wood and paper industries and companies).

Chips can come from lumber mills or from processors that grind trees to chips immediately after harvesting (Chapter 4). Chips are generally sold by the "green ton," or by volume in "units" (see "Wood chip basics" on page 31).

A mill's chip storage and unloading area will usually be served by a track or tracks separate from the roundwood area. Upon arrival, chips must be unloaded from their cars. There are five main methods: Bottom-dumping cars discharging into a between-rails pit, where chips enter a conveyor; rotary dumping; end dumping; mechanical unloading (overhead bucket or a front-end loader that enters the car via an end door); and vacuum (pneumatic). Each mill has a preferred method.

There are exceptions, but mills in the West and Northwest generally prefer gondola-style cars for end, rotary, or mechanical dumping, while Eastern mills — which have fewer issues with snow and frozen loads — favor hopper-style cars with bottom dumping.

Rotary and end dumping require a switching move for each car to place it on or in the dumper (and end dumping for cars with only one end door may have to be turned on a wye). Bottom-dump, mechanical, and pneumatic unloading may have multiple spots along a track allowing two or more cars to be unloaded before moving them.

Trucks are unloaded in the same area. End-dump ramps that elevate the entire truck are common; others unload via bottom dump outlets in the trailer.

Most mills have multiple chip piles. Some have one for hardwood and one for softwood; chips will be divided by age as well, as mills generally process them in first-in, first-out order. Mills usually move chips with belt conveyors,

A bulk semi makes a delivery to the chemical receiving area at the Plainwell Paper Co., in Plainwell, Mich. Mills have a variety of tanks for holding various chemicals and additives; also note the water tower in the background painted with the mill name and logo. Jim Hediger

but some use pneumatic pipe systems. Conveyors are the most energy efficient to use, but are more expensive to install. Tall auger-style conveyors can also be used. The ground under chip piles is usually paved, which aids drainage and keeps chips from being contaminated with dirt and debris when being handled.

Wood chip piles can be 50 feet or taller in height (and include up to 25,000 tons of chips), although some companies (and local laws) establish limits for safety, for both fire risk and worker safety from pile instability.

The conventional method of working the chip pile is with a conveyor running next to the chip piles just below ground level. A bulldozer shoves chips into the conveyor, which carries chips to the mill. Piles are worked from one end to another to make sure chips are used in order, so the oldest chips are used first.

Some modern plants instead use a rotating auger-style "reclaim system" under the chip pile. This takes a supply of chips evenly from the bottom of the pile, allowing new chips to be continually added directly atop the pile. Although more expensive to install, it eliminates the need for a bulldozer to continually work the pile.

Outbound loads can also be generated from these tracks. Waste such as bark, sawdust (too fine to process as pulp), and other wood pieces unsuitable for processing are often burned as fuel on site. This material can also be sold and shipped, either by railcar (a chip car) or truck.

Chemical and material unloading and storage

Mills receive a great deal of chemicals and other additives by rail and truck. Chapter 8 includes a summary of these products, along with the types of freight cars that carried them in various eras. How you model this will depend on the size of your mill, what product it produces, and the time period.

For example, a 1940s mill producing coated paper would likely receive kaolin clay bagged in boxcars. In the 1960s the clay would likely be delivered in bulk in three-bay, 3,300- to 4,000-cubic-foot covered hoppers, and by the 1990s it would arrive in slurry form in 14,000-gallon tank cars.

Unloading and storage areas for inbound materials will be grouped by car type and product type: tank cars, covered hoppers (including pressure-differential pneumatic cars), and boxcars.

Boxcars will head to a warehouse building for unloading (depending upon the mill size, it may have separate warehouses for inbound and outbound loads). This could include bagged kaolin and starch, loads of market pulp, chemicals in steel or plastic drums, or bales of recycled paper.

Tank cars will be handled on a separate track or tracks near stationary storage tanks. The unloading area is often covered or inside a shed with a roll-up door. Inbound cars can include cars of chlorine, caustic soda, hydrogen peroxide, titanium dioxide slurry, kaolin clay slurry, limestone slurry, and sulfur or sulfuric acid. Outbound tanks include occasional cars of waste sludge or byproducts such as ammonia.

Covered hoppers may be handled in the same area as tank cars, but may have their own track and unloading area. This can be a between-the-rails pit and conveyor system for conventional cars, or a pneumatic (pipe) system for unloading pressure-differential cars and Airslide covered hoppers. Products in covered hoppers can include kaolin and other clays, starch, dolomite, lime, and soda ash.

These chemicals and additives are stored in tanks and bins, in a tremendous variety of shapes, styles, and sizes, all connected by a maze of piping. They're all usually located near and around the digester building (more on that in a bit).

Processing wood

The papermaking process begins with pulling bolts or wood chips from their storage piles. For pulpwood, this means a loader or bulldozer placing bolts on a conveyor that takes them to the grinder. The bolts travel upward into a mill building where the grinder is located (called the wood room or the chipper or grinder room). The multiple blades in the chipper grind the wood into small pieces to make it easier to separate the fiber.

Uniform size is very important for even cooking/processing, so chips are up to an inch long and no more than 3⁄16" thick. The chips are screened to separate sawdust and remove any stray material, then conveyed to storage bins (chip bins or silos). Depending upon the mill and era, the chips may

Chips are conveyed from the piles at left to the digester building at right at the Willamette mill. The pulp is piped from there to the papermaking building (behind the photographer). Chip truck unloading bays are at far left, with several trailers parked at center. Also note the high-voltage electrical switching yard at left. Jim Hediger

The papermaking machine at the Willamette mill is in the long, low building, marked by steam from multiple vents. Covered hoppers are unloaded at left (behind the row of boxcars). The track at right enters the warehouse through a roll-up door. Truck scales are at bottom, leading to the chip unloading area. Jim Hediger

Boxed products on pallets (left) and paper rolls (right) await shipping. Jim Hediger

be heated to dry them and reduce the moisture content to make the pulping process more efficient.

The chip silos (they often look like grain silos, with a conical bottom) hold from 50-300 tons of chips, and are located on or in the digester building. A conveyor/turntable directly under the silo allows pulling chips from the bottom, where they're taken to the digester. Chips pulled from outside storage piles are conveyed and screened, just like chips produced from on-site grinding.

Multiple chip bins or surge bins may be used, with each holding a different species of wood. This allows them to be metered out and blended before moving on to the next step, when the chips head to the digester.

Pulp is usually stored in tall concrete tanks or vessels. Jim Hediger

Digester building

The building housing the digesters — large vertical vessels that can be 70 feet or taller — is generally the tallest building at the mill. Depending upon the era and mill capacity, this building can be from four to 10 stories tall. It will be marked by lots of piping and connections to any outdoor chemical storage tanks and to buildings housing the paper machines. The building may house multiple digesters and related processing equipment, which is all out of sight from viewers.

Once the pulp is made, it is stored in large storage tanks (concrete at modern mills) until it is needed to make stock for the paper machine, or it's processed into sheets or rolls of pulp for either long-term storage or shipping to another mill.

A key part of recovering and recycling materials used in the digesters at kraft mills is the lime kiln. After the black liquor is processed following the cooking process, a portion of it is reacted with quicklime and burned in a rotary lime kiln. This reburned lime is then reused in the cooking process ("recausticizing"). The kiln is a long, low, horizontal tube or barrel sitting at an angle. As it rotates, the materials inside move from top to bottom, under intense heat as they travel. The kiln is a prominent feature of many prototype mills, but since it's not directly rail served, it's often a detail best left off of a modeled scene.

Recycled paper can also be processed in the digester building. Paper was being recycled by World War II, and the amount of paper saved for recycling has increased dramatically in the past few decades. Wood fibers can be reused several times, and it's easier and cheaper to reclaim fibers from recycled paper than raw wood.

Recycled paper is collected and sorted at reclamation centers. It is then baled by type and shipped to mills in trucks or general-purpose boxcars — it sometimes arrives as a backhaul in a newsprint-service boxcar. The amount of recycled paper used varies by mill.

The inbound paper goes to a vessel where it is chemically and mechanically deinked, and depending upon its final intended use, bleached. It is then pulped in much the same way as wood chips, but an advantage is that it takes less energy and chemicals to separate fibers from paper than from wood. The resulting pulp is then mixed with pulp from other processes, again depending upon the final use for the paper.

The pulp is then blended as needed to make stock, the liquid used by paper-making machines to create the finished products of the mill. The stock is piped to the building housing the paper machine.

Paper machine building

The biggest piece of machinery, and the largest investment at a mill, is the paper machine itself. Modern machines typically stretch 300 feet or more in length, and the building housing the machine (or machines) will be even longer. Although the building will not be as tall as the digester building, a modern machine can stand three or more stories tall, so the paper-making building will often be 30 to 40 feet tall.

Many mills have indoor loading tracks, with concrete platforms at car-floor level. Steel bridge plates in the door openings allow lift trucks to enter cars. Jim Hediger

Lift trucks with paper-roll clamps load and unload boxcars and trailers. They enable rolls to be moved and stacked with a great deal of control. Jim Hediger

Along with its long profile, you can usually easily spot this building by the multiple vents that emit a heavy output of steam from the paper drying process. A mill having multiple machines may have them both in the same building; however, if they were installed at different times, it's likely they're in separate buildings.

An early forklift loads wrapped bundles of kraft paper at a Houston mill in 1943. Tight doorways and weak floors limited forklift access on early boxcars. The sign at left says "LOOK OUT FOR JITNEYS." John Vachon, Library of Congress

Warehouse and shipping

As the paper emerges from the paper machine it's taken up in large rolls. These are taken to the rewind area, which can be attached to the paper-making building or the warehouse, which is usually attached for convenience. These rolls are unwound, cut to the widths needed by customers, and rewound to the prescribed length. These cut rolls are then wrapped (either in paper or in plastic), labeled with a product number, weight, and description, and stored in the warehouse until they're shipped.

Paper can also be sheeted — cut into sheets and stored flat. Depending upon the mill, this can mean large pallet-sized sheets destined for further processing, or paper can be trimmed to final size (reams of 8½x11 copier paper, for example), packaged, and put into cartons on pallets for shipping. Larger mills often ship rolls or large sheets to separate plants that process the paper into final products.

Warehouses are large structures, usually one or two stories tall. They are temperature and humidity controlled, as paper is sensitive to these conditions. Various areas will be dedicated to the products produced: rolls of various sizes, sheets of paper and card on pallets, and cases of finished products on pallets. Depending upon the size of the operation, a mill may have a separate warehouse for inbound materials (such as bales of pulp or recycled paper).

One or more tracks will serve the warehouse. The track can be inside the building (common in areas with harsh weather), or at an outside dock that's covered — again, protecting finished paper from the elements. Another option is a dock that's external, but covered by a shed (more extensive than a simple canopy, less expensive than running track indoors).

The warehouse, especially at modern mills, will also have extensive truck docks with multiple doors for loading semi trailers. There will also be a nearby lot for parking trailers awaiting loading and unloading, and likely a utility/dock tractor or two for moving trailers within the plant.

Paper rolls are carried by forklift-style trucks that have rounded clamps instead of forks. These secure the rolls and carry them vertically, allowing them to be stacked in warehouses as well as in boxcars and trailers. You'll see these trucks throughout the ware-

Two Blue Ridge Southern diesels spot a pair of boxcars along the dock at Jackson Paper Manufacturing at Sylva, N.C., on the former Southern Railway Murphy Branch, in 2016. The classic-styled mill (formerly owned by Mead) makes containerboard from 100% recycled paper, then ships it in rolls by rail and truck.
Jim Wrinn

The power plant at Champion Paper in Hamilton, Ohio, is a classic brick building that dominates the scene, top. The track snaking its way between buildings leads to the coal unloader, above. Note the blue flag protection, indicating the cars beyond aren't to be moved. A pair of 100-ton coal hoppers are visible in the distance.
Two photos: Jim Hediger

house, winding area, and on the docks where boxcars and trailers are loaded. Prior to the advent of these customized forklifts, rolls were moved by handcarts —you can see this in photos throughout the book.

Standard forklifts and pallet jacks move pallets of pulp, and cases of finished products, and miscellaneous other materials around the mill.

Power plant

The paper-making process requires a tremendous amount of energy. Mills have multiple large boilers to provide the massive amounts of steam required to power equipment and dry the paper. Many plants generated their own electricity as well, with all of this equipment housed in a substantial structure called a power plant.

Their appearance is much like a municipal power plant. Brick construction was typical through the steam era, with the power plant building marked by a tall smokestack. Concrete has become the preferred material for newer power-plant buildings.

Coal was commonly used through the steam era, but environmental concerns and stricter pollution regulations led to other fuels, and to the use of scrubbers and other advanced emission-control equipment to limit pollutants at plants that continued to burn coal.

Fuel oil was a popular early alternate to coal, especially through the 1950s. This was often in the form of No. 6 fuel oil ("Bunker C"), a heavy, thick substance that required heating to flow properly for unloading and use. The use of fuel oil dropped in the following decade as prices increased and Bunker C became a popular feedstock for petrochemicals.

Liquified petroleum gas (LPG) emerged as an industrial fuel starting in the 1930s, and its clean-burning properties helped increase its popularity, especially for rural and small-town mills. Some mills burn natural gas (received by pipeline), which is most common in the South and Southeast.

Many mills have boilers that can burn multiple types of fuel, allowing mills to react to market prices and availability. Mills also burn waste products as fuel, including unpulpable wood scraps, bark, sawdust, and in recent decades, spent pulping liquor and sludge.

Rail service to the power plant depends upon the type of fuels being used. Coal-fired plants have a trestle or receiving track over receiving bins, conveyors, or piles. A mill could receive several cars per day, typically in 50- or 70-ton bottom-dump hoppers. From the 1960s onward, coal unloading areas were more likely to be covered. Car size increased, with 100-ton hoppers starting in the 1960s and 110-ton cars by the late 1990s. (A baseline for estimating coal use is 1.5 tons of coal per 1 ton of paper produced.)

The spur serving the coal unloader needs room to spot the loaded cars at one end of the trestle or unloading bay, with enough room for cars to be moved and unloaded during the day. Once loads were spotted, they are often moved by a car puller or portable car mover.

Plants using fuel oil or LPG would have trackside pipe connections for tank cars — usually ground-level pipes to connect to bottom outlets for fuel oil, and high-mounted flexible hoses to connect to fittings in the housings atop LPG tank cars. Tracks should have room for multiple cars.

Mills on rivers would sometimes have a neighboring dam for producing hydroelectric power. The generators and other electrical equipment would be housed in a brick building adjoining the dam.

Other mill details and features

The water treatment plant is a feature that falls into the category of being extremely important to a prototype mill, but low priority for modeling. The tremendous amount of water used at a paper mill — much of which was once discharged directly back into neighboring rivers and lakes — is now treated. This will include a series of tanks and holding ponds, with buildings including a sludge effluent plant and clarifier. It looks like a municipal water treatment plant.

Roadways and paths snake throughout the plant. These were often dirt and gravel through the steam era, but are now usually paved. Large employee parking lots will be nearby, with smaller lots for company and service vehicles within the mill complex.

Fencing for security is also now common, with chain link topped with barbed wire around the entire mill area. Gates with security booths are located at entrances, with separate entrances for trucks and employees.

The mill will have one or more large elevated water towers (much like a town's municipal water tower) to ensure a ready supply of water under pressure. Since they're prominent, these towers often carry the mill name and logo on their sides.

An office building will be near the main entrance, which may or may not be physically part of another plant building. Signs on or near this building may carry the full company name and logo; signs can also be on any tall building facing public view. Old signs may also still be visible. For example, signs on smokestacks were common, often done as part of the brick design, and may reflect a name or owner that hasn't existed for decades.

Rail yard and track

Central to our interests is the railroad trackage that extends through the mill. We've seen how rail serves various areas of the plant, but how it all comes together is unique to each mill. Large mills will have a holding yard where the serving railroad drops off and picks up large cuts of cars. Tracks extend from there to various areas; there may be a main track looping around the complex, while a mill with a narrow footprint will have multiple tracks snaking among buildings.

Chapters 9 and 10 provide details on mill trackage, train operations, and how to effectively model them. As you can see, there's a tremendous range of possibilities for modeling, regardless of the era and region. Chapter 10 takes a closer look at some specific models available, with ideas on capturing mills in limited space and track plans featuring large and small mills.

A Mississippi Export General Electric 44-tonner pulls a string of boxcars from the Southern Paper mill at Moss Point, Miss., in 1941. General Electric

Truck loading docks are prominent at mills. Trailers may wear paint schemes of the paper company (as here, with Appleton Papers), leasing company, or other trucking line. Jim Hediger

Georgia-Pacific has its name prominently displayed on a tall building at its Kalamazoo, Mich., mill, as well as the office building at the main entrance and a separate sign near the street. Jim Hediger

CHAPTER FOUR

PULP AND WOOD CHIP LOADING FACILITIES

Pulpwood logs and wood chips come from a variety of sources. Their sorting yards and railcar loading areas lend themselves well to modeling, and you don't need to have an on-line paper mill to model a pulpwood or chip loadout facility.

The conveyor and chip loader at Bristol Industries' loadout at Bridgewater, N.C., can deliver chips into railcars on two tracks as well as to truck trailers (near side). A car puller moves cars during loading; empties are held in storage tracks to the right. The operation on Norfolk Southern is shown circa 2000. Kyle Lael

Options for modern-day modelers are fewer than those for modelers of the steam era through the 1970s. Although some pulpwood and chips still travel by rail (12,000 pulpwood loads and 40,000 chip loads in 2019), the number of rail loading facilities has dropped significantly over the past few decades, as trucks have captured the vast majority of the traffic.

Through the steam and early diesel eras, however, rail loadouts were common in forested areas. A pulpwood loading area could be as simple as a team track at a small-town station holding a single car or two, or a short spur in a rural area or small town. It could also be a large sorting yard that covers several acres, with multiple tracks allowing several cars to be loaded.

Wood chip operations began in the 1940s. Through the 1950s, these were residual chips as a byproduct from sawmills. Since the 1960s, chips have been ground from whole trees and shipped directly to paper mills.

Both types of operations provide a great opportunity to add an industry or two, along with some varied equipment, to a layout of almost any size. These industries also provide operational challenges that come with running specialized equipment, such as the reduced speeds required of trains carrying many types of pulpwood cars (more on that in Chapter 9).

Pulpwood operations

Land being forested can be owned by a private individual, a corporation, or a mill/paper/lumber company. It can also be owned by the state or federal government, under lease to a company or private individual. The size and scope of each operation, and the details of how the wood is handled, depends upon the size of the forest being worked and the era.

A small operation on a few acres of private land may involve just a couple of workers felling trees, cutting logs to length, and moving them trackside by wagon or truck. A large corporate operation will have multiple crews and vehicles, with a large area to sort and stack wood for loading to railcars.

Small operations were more common through the steam era. As mills shrank in number and grew in size (and machines became larger and more efficient), large-scale mechanized harvesting became more common. Small operations tended to be labor intensive, with logs moved stick by stick from truck to storage to railcar. Larger operations were heavily mechanized, and as cutting and loading equipment improved and became larger, the big operations dominated by the 1960s.

How trees are harvested depends upon the wood type, the size and age of the trees, and whether an area is being clear-cut or thinned. Lumberjacks with saws and axes in the 1800s largely gave way to power saws and cutters by the early 1900s for large operations.

Trees and timber are sorted, with the best destined to become lumber ("sawlogs") and lower-quality or excess trees cut for pulp. Land covered largely by scrub and low-quality trees might all be destined for pulp, while land with high-value timber might have crews clearing just low-value pulp logs.

For pulpwood, this means that as soon as trees are felled, workers trim branches. The logs are then cut into shorter sections ("bolts") of a specific length. Four feet was common for bolts carried in boxcars or on pulpwood flatcars, where they were stacked in two rows along the deck. Some operations and mills specified longer bolts (4'-6" or 5'-0"), a length that could still be moved by hand by a pair of workers.

By the 1960s some mills called for bolts 8 feet long, enabled by mechanized loading and unloading. This saved labor, requiring less cutting. Paper mills today often receive tree-length logs, with size limited by truck trailer length and railcar size (two longitudinal stacks on a bulkhead car with side stakes).

The process of getting the bolts from the forest or cutting area to trackside evolved by era and accessibility. Sleds were common in many areas through the 1940s, especially during winter months. Horse-drawn wagons were also used well into the internal-combustion era, especially in areas where space was tight and ground was soft.

Trucks have been used for pulpwood logging since the 1920s. Straight trucks and trailers were modified with skeleton frames to reduce weight and allow carrying as much wood as possible. Their size and specific design varied, depending if they traveled only on private roads or if they also used public roadways.

Through the steam era, these trucks were often older models, and could be quite beat-up because of their service — especially on older, smaller operations. Larger corporate operations were more likely to have newer, larger trucks that were purpose-built for their service.

Small operations would bring logs trackside, either to a team track or spur near the logging area. A logging company might lease space on a spur serving other industries or businesses. These provide ways of modeling pulp operations without significant change to a layout.

Logs would be transloaded directly from the truck to a railcar. The local railroad clerk ordered the car or cars as needed. This avoided the need for a storage area, and minimized labor requirements (saving handling logs multiple times by storing them). Workers loaded railcars by hand, stack-

Horse-drawn sleds were commonly used to get logs (bolts) from cutting areas to truck or rail loadouts, especially in winter, in some areas into the 1940s. At top, horses drag eight-foot bolts along a muddy path to a loading area near Effie, Minn., in September 1937. Above, a worker loads a sled on a snowy February day in 1936 in Coos County, New Hampshire. Top: Russell Lee, Library of Congress; Above: Arthur Rothstein, Library of Congress

ing logs one by one.

A slightly larger operation might work in similar fashion, but have a small storage area so that logs could be gathered at trackside before railcars were ordered. Although this required more labor, it allowed two or three railcars to be loaded at once.

A large dedicated pulpwood lot will have a significant amount of storage area for stacking wood. The wood will also be sorted by type, if multiple species were being cut. It will have a dedicated rail spur, perhaps with multiple tracks, with space to spot several cars.

Trucks bringing their loads to the lot will be mechanically unloaded, and railcars will also be loaded mechanically. Specific equipment varied, but as the photos on following pages show, it was typically done by tractors with large C-shaped claws that can scoop multiple logs at once. These mechanical loaders greatly improved efficiency, but their cost meant a greater volume of logs were required as well, which meant larger facilities.

A pulpwood yard will typically have a guardhouse or office at the entrance for trucks to check in and out (perhaps with a gate). A maintenance building or shed would also be common. The yard may or may not be fenced, depending upon era and location.

Gravel surfaces and paths would run throughout, with rows of pulpwood stacks, with logs uniformly cut to the lengths specified by customers.

Rail operations would involve a local freight stopping to pull loaded cars and spot empties to replace them. Cars are generally left in place for loading, with the mechanical loader moving from car to car along the tracks. A derail will be located on the spur near where it meets the main track.

Loaded cars must meet clearances — many pulpwood flat cars include stenciling warning specific limits on ends of logs overhanging the car sides. Pulpwood yards sometimes have mechanical devices to help with this. The photo on page 50 shows a yard in North Carolina with a home-built "load straightener" made from a pair of old pneumatic brake cylinders and large steel sheets that press the logs firmly to the center of the car. Loaded cars will be pulled through the straightener as needed, adding a step to train operations.

Pulpwood trucks are loaded from storage stacks near cutting areas in rural Littleton, N.H., in February 1940. Trucks can carry logs either to rail loading areas or directly to mills, depending upon distance. Marion Post Wolcott, Library of Congress

Pulpwood bolts are cut to specific lengths as called for by individual mills. Here a logger uses a standard pole as a guide to mark a bolt with an axe. Russell Lee, Library of Congress

Wood chip loadouts

Chips are a more modern traffic source. Through the 1950s, chips came mainly from lumber mills as a residual product (cleaned chips for pulp; bark and other waste as "hog fuel"). By the 1960s, however, some companies were setting up chipping operations at the source of the timber, grinding entire trees and transporting chips instead of logs directly to paper mills.

Many of these modern chipping operations are 100% served by truck, but some still have rail operations for longer hauls.

Tree-length logs will arrive via truck at the yard. They will be sorted by wood type and by their suitability for lumber. Lumber-quality logs will be set aside for shipping to a sawmill (this sorting may also be done at the cutting area, with the chipping yard only receiving logs destined for pulp).

Logs are then handled in much the same way as at a mill. They're cut to the necessary length to go into the debarker (usually around 15 feet for a modern machine). The debarked logs are then run through the chipper; the chips are then cleaned, sorted, and screened.

Outbound products include the

Workers move pulpwood bolts from a truck to a boxcar at San Augustine, Texas, in 1943. Boxcars were commonly used to carry pulpwood from cutting areas to mills into the 1930s, with some operations continuing later. John Vachon, Library of Congress

cleaned and screened chips; the bark chips; and waste and residue from the screening process. The bark can be sold by itself as landscaping or fuel, or it can be combined with the other waste material as hog fuel. All of these will be stockpiled nearby to be loaded onto railcars or trucks for shipping to final customers.

Rail-served chip yards will have a long track or tracks to hold cars for loading. Loading varies by facility. Some have a simple conveyor that carries chips from ground level up to the cars. Larger loadouts are more likely to have overhead conveyors or pneumatic systems at car-height level, or perhaps an overhead surge bin.

Most loadouts require cars to be moved under the loader. It's not practical for a local freight to spot individual cars as they're loaded — the freight will pick up cuts of loaded cars and drop off empties — and most chip operations are small enough that they don't rate having their own switch engine.

The typical solution for this is to use

Railroads in the Upper Midwest favored gondolas for pulpwood loading. Two workers move eight-foot debarked bolts from a truck into a New York Central gondola on the Chicago & North Western in the tiny town of Springbrook, Wis., in 1941. John Vachon, Library of Congress

Pulpwood racks — flatcars with angled decks and bulkheads — became the most popular car for hauling bolts in the South, East, and Northeast, as they could be loaded and unloaded manually or mechanically. Here a truckload of four-foot logs is transloaded near Nacogdoches, Texas, in 1943. John Vachon, Library of Congress

a car puller, a stationary device with a rotating cylinder around which a cable, attached to a car, is wound. Another method is to have the track on a slight grade to allow cars to roll into position, with a worker riding a car and using handbrakes to control movement. If this is done, the slope will be away from the main line. (For modeling, we generally want to keep tracks level to avoid accidental movement.) And as with the pulpwood yard spur, there will be a derail on the spur near where it connects with the main track.

Loads in wood chip cars can be piled to varying heights depending upon the length of travel, route clearances, and the specifications of the final customer. (Chapter 7 includes details on wood chip cars). Mesh nets are attached over the load to keep chips from blowing away.

As with a pulpwood yard, a chip yard will have an office or security building at the entry, likely gated. A scale and scalehouse for trucks will be on the entry road. The debarker and chipper will be similar to those at mills; a maintenance building will house repair and sharpening equipment. A large paved or graded lot will be needed for truck unloading and loading, and multiple semi trailers may be parked around the lot.

A model of a chip loadout operation can include some or all of this, or just focus on the rail loading area.

Southern Railway pulpwood cars, converted from old boxcars, await loading at the Robbinsville, N.C., wood yard on the Graham County Railroad in December 1974. A hydraulic lift on the front of a loader lifts logs to the cars. Two photos: Dan Ranger

A truck-mounted crane with claw attachment loads pulpwood logs onto cars at Cape Fear Wood Co., near Lumberton, N.C., in 1979. Another truck works in the distance at left. Mike Small

The guard shack/office at the pulpwood yard at Ehrhardt, S.C., in 1960 includes myriad details including signs, bench, Coke machine and crates, and a chain across the entrance. The yard was served by an Atlantic Coast Line branch. William S. Stokes

Today, trucks carry most pulpwood logs directly to mills. These semis are being weighed as they deliver logs to the Alabama River Pulp Co., at the Caiborne (Ala.) mill complex. George F. Landegger Collection of Alabama Photographs in Carol M. Highsmith's America, Library of Congress

This "pulpwood squeezer" is a homemade device to push logs into alignment on pulpwood cars. The air reservoir on the ground powers old brake cylinders behind the vertical pivoting sheets, which press the ends of the logs toward the center of the car, keeping them within clearance guidelines. William S. Stokes

The wood chip loader at the Androscoggin Corp., in Oakland, Maine, served by Maine Central, tops off converted Portland Terminal hopper cars in the early 1960s. The company processes waste lumber into chips. Car No. 110 is a three-bay steel hopper with wood plank side extensions; it stands 16'-4" tall and has a 4,846-cf capacity. *Trains* magazine collection

A lumber mill at Everett, Wash., loads scrap wood chips into a Great Northern car converted from an old 50-foot single-sheathed boxcar (4,704-cf capacity). The chips aren't suitable for pulping, so they're sold to mills as "hog fuel," destined for burning in mill boilers. Brotherhood of Locomotive Firemen and Enginemen

A Blue Ridge Southern train crew waits for a loader to clean the rails at a crossing before proceeding to pick up a pair of high-stacked chip loads from T&S Hardwoods at Addie, N.C. It's April 2016 on the former Southern Railway Murphy Branch. Jim Wrinn

Modern pulpwood trucks and cars are loaded by cranes and mechanized loaders. Tree-length logs are now common for pulpwood. This truck is being unloaded at Bristol Industries' chipping facility at Bridgewater, N.C. Kyle Lael

Wood chip cars are loaded at the Bristol Industries' loadout. As they're loaded, cars are pulled back (toward the camera) by the car puller, which sits between the tracks just beyond the fence. Kyle La

The truck loading area at at Bristol Industries includes a large gravel lot for parking chip trailers. Kyle Lael

At Bristol Industries' chip facility, a circular-mounted crane unloads trucks and feeds logs to the debarker (right). The circular rail upon which it travels is 132 feet in diameter. Logs are stored by species around the crane. Kyle Lael

CHAPTER FIVE

PAPER SERVICE BOXCARS

By the late 1970s, Canadian Pacific was painting its dedicated newsprint cars green, with the small "Newsprint Service Only" shield on the right side. This 50-foot plug-door, external-post boxcar, built by National Steel Car, was just two months old in this December 1977 photo. The CPI reporting marks (and additional stenciling) indicated the car was in international service. R.J. Wilhelm; Jeff Wilson collection

Boxcars have been railroads' primary method of carrying finished paper products since the early days of paper mill operations in the 1800s. They have evolved in size and features since the steam era, and choosing the proper cars for this service will result in more realistic operations around modeled paper mills.

Through the 1950s, any clean Class A boxcar could be used for newsprint or paper loading. This Canadian National 40-foot single-sheathed car is stenciled "THIS CAR FOR CLEAN LADING ONLY." It was built in 1931 and later rebuilt and repainted; this photo is from September 1960. John Ingles; Jeff Wilson collection

This steel 40-foot boxcar, photographed in 1961, is typical of Canadian cars used for newsprint from the 1940s through the 1960s. It's one of the first steel cars bought by Canadian National, built in December 1937 by NSC. The AAR-design car has NSC ends, Hutchins roof, and Youngstown doors. It's stenciled "THIS CAR FOR CLEAN LADING ONLY." John Ingles; Jeff Wilson collection

This Canadian Pacific 40-foot steel car is stenciled "TO BE USED EXCLUSIVELY FOR NEWSPRINT, PAPER, FLOUR, AND SUGAR OR HIGH-CLASS MERCHANDISE." It was built in May 1951 and was photographed in October 1963. John Ingles; Jeff Wilson collection

Paper — namely newsprint — cars can be a key element on layouts of all modelers, regardless of the railroad or region you model. Other freight cars related to the industry were either local to the mill (pulpwood, wood chip) or tended to stick to specific regions or routes (chemical, slurry). Paper cars, however, carried finished products such as rolls of newsprint from U.S. and Canadian mills to newspaper presses, printers, and other final users throughout North America. The challenge in modeling them is that they often look like other general-service boxcars, blending into freight trains. There are ways to distinguish them and help set them apart.

Paper car basics

Rolls of newsprint are difficult to handle because of their bulk, shape, and heavy weight (often a thousand pounds or more), and they are easily damaged. And what might initially seem like minor damage can make an entire roll of paper unfit for use on a printing press. Common railcar- and

This yellow Toronto, Hamilton & Buffalo car carries the same lading stenciling as the CP car on page 55. It was built by NSC in 1953; it's shown here in August 1958. The TH&B was co-owned by the Canadian Pacific and New York Central.
John Ingles; Jeff Wilson collection

In 1961, Canadian Pacific ordered 1,150 new boxcars exclusively for newsprint service. The 40-foot cars, with eight-foot sliding doors, bore a distinctive red shield with "Newsprint Service Only" lettering. Number 58480 was built by NSC.
Canadian Pacific

Canadian National in 1960 began assigning groups of boxcars to newsprint service, painting the doors yellow and stenciling them (also see the label on the upper tack board). Note the cardboard tacked vertically inside the door edges to protect against leaks.
Canadian National

handling-related damage with paper rolls includes:

• Water (caused by leaking roofs or doors that didn't seal tightly)

• Gouges (from improper handling or protruding fasteners in cars)

• Flat spots (at the end of a roll, from excessive or forceful contact with the base of car interior walls or ends)

• Edge damage (from improper handling, sliding on the floor, or being tipped/leaned on edge)

• Chaffing (from repeated movement or sliding contact with rough car interior walls or adjoining paper rolls)

• Out-of-round rolls/crushed cores (caused by improper loading or excessive slack or coupling forces)

Because of this, boxcars in paper service must be in excellent physical condition. By specific railroad standards, they should be Class A cars (see "Boxcar quality qualifications" on page 63). They should be weathertight, with roofs, walls, floors, and doors that are sealed and allow no leaks.

The interior walls and floor must be smooth — a single stray nail or bolt protruding from a wall or left from blocking a previous load on the floor can easily cause thousands of dollars in damage and ruin multiple paper rolls. Car lining can be wood planks, plywood, composite, epoxy-lined, or other material, as long as it is smooth.

The standards for paper loads are similar to other loads that railroads define as "clean lading." Along with paper, this means loads such as food products and beverages in cases as well as other boxed consumer goods (everything from paper plates and dog food to shoes and clothing).

Early boxcars had standard sliding doors, but these tended to leak after repeated use, so weren't ideal. Plug doors emerged in the 1950s, first on refrigerator cars and then on insulated boxcars. Although a more expensive option, they became preferred for paper loads as they provide a tight seal. Wider door openings were also preferable for paper loads. A six-foot door width was standard for general-purpose boxcars of the steam era, but wider doors made it easier to maneuver bulky paper rolls into place and allowed access for forklifts. Floors on these wide-door cars needed to be strong enough to hold forklifts and powered loaders.

A feature not required but certainly preferred was a car with a cushion underframe. These (either through-sill or end-sill designs) absorb shock from coupling and slack action, helping protect paper rolls from shifting during transport. These forces can slam rolls together or force them hard to the walls or ends, which can cause flat spots or even force a roll out of round.

Steam era

Cars dedicated specifically to paper and newsprint loads were rare through the steam and early diesel eras, and didn't begin appearing in large numbers until the late 1950s and early 1960s. Until that period, for the most part, railroads would use any clean Class A car that was available. Since general-service boxcars were by far the most common car type, appropriate cars were generally readily available.

Railroads would follow car service rules regarding car selection: For loads going offline, first preference was a car owned by the railroad of the receiving customer; next would be cars owned by railroads in the direction of the receiver; and finally cars of the shipping railroad.

The boxcar interior photo on page 62 shows a typical rolled paper load of the steam era. That car (St. Louis-San Francisco No. 148032) is a single-sheathed wood (steel-frame) car with wood doors and steel ends. It wasn't in assigned service — it was simply a car graded Class A that was suitable for a paper load on the day it was assigned to the Southland paper mill in Lufkin, Texas.

The Canadian National boxcar shown on the top of page 55 is another example. It's not solely for paper, but is stenciled "THIS CAR FOR CLEAN LADING ONLY," so the railroad is trying to keep it in Class A condition.

Mills would sometimes add extra material (tape and filler) around door edges on cars with doors that might not seal properly. Examples can be seen in the photo on page 28 in Chapter 3.

Canadian National No. 485491 was built by NSC in 1944 and refurbished in January 1961, receiving the yellow door indicating newsprint service. It's rolling in a Wabash train in April 1961. John Ingles; Jeff Wilson collection

Canadian National newsprint cars were common sights in U.S. trains. Eastern Car Co. built this car, which was rebuilt with an eight-foot door in 1966. It received the "noodle" logo and yellow newsprint door; it's shown here in 1971. Jeff Wilson collection

Bangor & Aroostook No. 10220 is one of 350 50-foot cars with nine-foot doors built by ACF in 1957. The cars received BAR's distinctive red, white, and blue scheme with stenciling "FOR NEWSPRINT LOADING, RETURN HOME PROMPTLY." The car is shown in 1959. John Ingles; Jeff Wilson collection

Bangor & Aroostook No. 2099, an insulated/heated 40-foot plug-door car built for potato service, wears stenciling for newsprint service in November 1961. Note the BAR's unique newsprint tag — shaped like a paper roll — on the tack board. John Ingles; Jeff Wilson collection

Pullman-Standard built this 50-foot PS-1 boxcar for its Transport Leasing Co. fleet in 1962. It's leased by Spruce Falls Power & Paper Co., Ltd., to carry newsprint. The cushion-underframe car, with an eight-foot door, is shown in 1966. Jeff Wilson collection

This 50-foot Transport Leasing Co. (Pullman-Standard) PS-1 boxcar has a plug door. One of a 20-car series (Nos. 40-59), it's assigned to a newsprint shipper on Canadian Pacific in 1963. J. David Ingles

National Steel Car built this 50-foot car for Pacific Great Eastern in January 1966. It has a nine-foot plug door, 11-foot interior height, and is labeled for paper service (under the herald). It's five months old in this May 1966 photo. John Ingles; Jeff Wilson collection

Dedicated newsprint cars

The Bangor & Aroostook was an early railroad that by the 1940s had a couple of groups of boxcars dedicated to newsprint service (specified by a "paper" notation in the *Official Railway Equipment Register*). This included early wood cars (Nos. 61000-61599) and steel cars (65000-65649), all 40-footers. The steel cars, built by Magor in the early 1940s, had special flooring (spruce over a yellow pine subfloor) for smoothness and strength. The cars served a large paper mill at Millinocket, Maine, which was the railroad's largest customer.

Other railroads would soon follow suit. By the late 1950s, the North American boxcar fleet (especially general-purpose cars) was beginning to shrink. Specialized cars were appearing for many types of lading once carried in general-service (AAR class XM) boxcars, a trend that would accelerate into the 1960s: insulated boxcars for many types of food products; specially equipped boxcars (with internal load restraint devices) for appliances and many consumer and industrial products; covered hoppers for many materials once hauled in bulk or bags in boxcars (cement, flour, sugar, and soon, grain); and bulkhead flats for bundled lumber.

Some railroads found it challenging to have enough Class A general-purpose cars on hand for newsprint and other rolled-paper service, so several began assigning specific groups of cars to carry paper. This was mainly done by railroads in Canada and the northern U.S. that served a large number of paper mills: Bangor & Aroostook; Canadian National; Canadian Pacific; Central Vermont; Duluth, Winnipeg & Pacific; Pacific Great Eastern (later BC Rail); Southern Pacific; Toronto, Hamilton & Buffalo; and Western Pacific all designated cars for paper service at some point.

In some cases these were groups of new cars specifically built for newsprint service; in others, older cars were rebuilt or reconditioned. How this designation was indicated varied widely depending upon the railroad or private owner. This could be simple stenciling (such as "NEWSPRINT LOADING ONLY" or "FOR PAPER SERVICE ONLY"), a larger logo or herald, or a variation of a paint scheme (car color or door color).

Among the first major railroads to do this were Canadian Pacific and Canadian National, both of which handled a tremendous amount of newsprint traffic heading from Canadian mills to U.S. printing plants.

In 1961, CP acquired the first cars of a 1,150-car order of 40-foot boxcars assigned exclusively to newsprint service. The cars, built by National Steel Car (NSC), had eight-foot-wide sliding doors and a 60-ton capacity (3,900-cubic-foot interior space). The railroad gave these cars an easy-to-spot red shield to the left of the door that included "NEWSPRINT SERVICE ONLY" lettering. At the same time, CP also rebuilt another 2,850 cars from older 40-foot cars and assigned them to newsprint service as well.

Canadian National had a huge fleet of 40-foot boxcars (more than 42,000 built to AAR standard designs from 1937 to 1956). It began assigning groups of these cars to newsprint service around 1960, indicating the service by painting the doors yellow (the bodies were boxcar red) with stenciling. The color coding would follow on newsprint cars of CN subsidiary railroads (CV and DW&P) through the 1980s, making these cars stand out in trains.

Keep in mind that the number of cars needed for paper (particularly newsprint), especially in Canada, extended far beyond cars assigned and labeled as such. Canadian National's boxcar fleet for many years was second only to the Pennsylvania Railroad's in number, and Canadian Pacific had the fourth-largest North American fleet. During the heyday of the 40-foot boxcar, you would be hard-pressed to spot a manifest freight in the U.S. that didn't include a Canadian car — which was most likely carrying paper.

South of the border, Bangor & Aroostook added to its earlier 40-foot newsprint cars with groups of 50-foot boxcars with nine-foot sliding doors, all painted in its famous red, white, and blue "State of Maine Products" scheme. The cars were built by ACF in 1957 (350 cars) and Pullman-Standard in 1962 (60 cars).

The BAR also assigned some of its insulated/heated potato-service plug-door boxcars (AAR class XIH) to newsprint service in the off-season as well. Car No. 2099, shown in page 58, displays the railroad's unique label on its tack board to indicate a newsprint load: a white tag resembling a vertical paper roll.

Pullman-Standard in the 1960s operated a small fleet of cars in its Transport Leasing fleet for paper service. These 50-foot PS-1 cars carried TLCX reporting marks. Some had logos of their lessees (including the Spruce Falls car on page 58); others had large TLCX logos. These cars became part of CP's international fleet in the early 1970s.

Modern paper cars

By the mid-1960s, railroads were moving largely to new 50-foot boxcar designs for most services. Railroads continued to invest in new newsprint cars, and among the most popular was a design introduced by NSC in 1966. The 50-foot, 70-ton car had a 9-foot plug door and an 11'-0" inside height,

Boxcars assigned to paper or newsprint service carry stenciling that can also include routing information. The note on this Western Pacific 50-foot, double-door boxcar specifies empty routing to the Great Northern in Portland, Ore. *Trains* Magazine collection

Duluth, Winnipeg & Pacific followed the lead of parent Canadian National in painting newsprint-service boxcar doors yellow. The NSC-built 50-foot, plug-door boxcar was a common newsprint car, and was purchased by several railroads. This car was just a year old when photographed in 1970. J. David Ingles

Minnesota, Dakota & Western No. 7092 is another NSC-built 50-foot plug-door newsprint car. The four-mile Minnesota short line, owned by Boise Cascade, rostered 100 of these cars (Nos. 7000-7099), built in 1969. J. David Ingles

Rolls of pulp await unloading from a 50-foot Railbox boxcar at a paper mill in the 1990s. Jim Hediger

PULP CARS

Along with newsprint and other finished paper products, boxcars are often used to transport rolls and bales or sheets of market pulp. These loads don't require the same level of care as finished products, since the pulp is destined to go into the vat at the mill upon delivery.

These cars represent inbound loads at paper mills. If the cars aren't suitable for carrying finished paper rolls, they'll simply leave the plant as empties after they're unloaded.

Newsprint-quality cars, however, also sometimes transport pulp. An assigned newsprint car (or a suitable Class A car) upon delivering a load of pulp will — after a thorough cleaning — sometimes be used for an outbound load of paper.

In 1970, Canadian National painted one of its 50-foot newsprint cars in a special scheme featuring banners of 20 Canadian newspapers. The scheme (which only appeared on one side of the car) was soon revised to include a narrow band at the bottom that included reporting marks and dimensional data. Canadian National

The Berlin Mills Railway was an example of a railroad owned by the paper manufacturer (Brown Co.) that also owned the mills it served around Berlin, N.H. The 50-foot incentive-per-diem (IPD) boxcar, one of 300 leased by the railroad, was built by Pacific Car & Foundry in 1979. R.J. Wilhelm; Jeff Wilson collection

This NSC 50-foot Central Vermont car built and shown in 1969 displays the Canadian National family newsprint scheme with a yellow door. The CVC reporting marks indicate CV cars built in Canada and assigned to international service. Jeff Wilson collection

By the 1980s and '90s, excess-height 50-foot cars were becoming more common in newsprint and paper service. This Southern Pacific double-plug-door, external-post car, built in 1985 and stenciled "FOR PAPER LOADING ONLY," was photographed in 1994. Jeff Wilson

Trailer Train pool boxcars, like this FBOX 50-foot, excess-height car built by Gunderson, are among the most common paper carriers in the 2020s. Jeff Wilson

Trailer Train's 60-foot TBOX cars, like this Trinity-built car, are often used for paper. However, clearance issues prevent some mills and customers from using the cars. Jeff Wilson

allowing many types of rolls to be loaded in two layers. Early versions of this car had smooth sides (interior posts), while later versions had vertical exterior posts (see the CP car on page 54). More than 3,500 would be built through 1971.

Several railroads purchased these cars, including CN, CP, CV, DW&P, Minnesota, Dakota & Western, and Pacific Great Eastern. All but the PGE cars had cushion underframes. Canadian National (and family roads CV and DW&P) continued identifying these newsprint cars by painting the door yellow. Canadian Pacific by the late 1960s was color-coding their boxcars — cars in newsprint service were green.

As in earlier eras, newsprint and paper still often traveled in general-service cars that weren't in dedicated service. This could be railroad-owned 50-foot cars with sliding or plug doors, and the incentive-per-diem (IPD) cars owned or leased by short lines that began appearing in large numbers in the mid-1970s. Some of these IPD cars were owned by railroads that owned or served paper mills. An example is the Berlin Mills Railway (page 60), which was owned by the paper company it served.

Railbox cars (single-door RBOX cars and combination plug/sliding-door ABOX cars) could be found hauling paper and pulp, especially when they were new and in reasonably good condition. Most of these were 70-ton capacity cars.

INTERNATIONAL AND DOMESTIC CARS AND SPECIAL REPORTING MARKS

Customs regulations during some periods of time sometimes complicated freight car use for paper loads crossing the U.S./Canadian border. For example, a Canadian-built car owned by a Canadian railroad could carry a load into the U.S. and be interchanged to a U.S. road; however, that car could not then be used to carry a domestic load from one U.S. point to another — it had to go directly back to Canada. (This is greatly simplified — regulations were far more complex than that, and were further complicated by Canadian railroads that had lines reaching into the U.S. and/or had U.S. subsidiary railroads.)

The "CPI" marks on this Canadian Pacific NSC-built 50-foot car indicate it is strictly for international shipments. Also note the newsprint service shield, the stencil regarding international service, and the card on the tack board reading "PAPER — DO NOT HUMP." Jeff Wilson collection

Cars assigned to cross-border traffic were sometimes stenciled to indicate this (such as "International Service Only"). To simplify this, Canadian National and Canadian Pacific both gave boxcars in this service unique reporting marks to make them readily identifiable to the services they were allowed to perform.

For CP, this included CPI (international) and CPAA (unrestricted American/U.S. use). For CN, this included CNIS (international), CNA (American), and for its subsidiaries, CVC (Central Vermont — Canadian) and DWC (Duluth, Winnipeg & Pacific — Canadian).

The restrictions were lifted around the time the U.S.-Canada Free Trade Agreement (1989) and North American Free Trade Agreement (1994) went into effect. Many cars subsequently had their reporting marks modified to the railroads' standard marks; others kept their reporting marks.

A boxcar has been loaded with rolls of newsprint at the Southland mill in Lufkin, Texas, in 1943. The St. Louis-San Francisco car is a single-sheathed, 40-foot Fowler boxcar with wood doors and a 50-ton capacity. In that era, any weathertight Class A boxcar could be used for paper service. John Vachon, Library of Congress

Paper rolls are loaded vertically in boxcars in one or two layers depending upon roll width and weight. Lift trucks with specially designed clamps carry the rolls. Canadian Pacific

Gaps between rolls at the middle of the car are filled to keep rolls from shifting. Since the 1970s, this is typically done with disposable inflatable dunnage (DID) bags. Kruger Publication Papers; *Trains* Magazine collection

MODELING

A number of manufacturers have offered models of AAR 40- and 50-foot boxcars along with 50-foot IPD and Railbox cars and 50- and 60-foot excess-height boxcars. In HO scale, Atlas and Walthers have offered versions of the NSC 50-foot newsprint cars, while Kaslo Shops makes a model of a Hawker-Siddeley newsprint car.

By the 1990s, boxcar numbers had dropped dramatically — from about 450,000 in service in 1977 to 190,000 by 1993, and down to 110,000 by 2024. A problem for shippers and railroads is that most of the 50-foot specialty and general-service cars used for paper in the 1970s have been retired, are about to be retired, or are no longer fit for paper service.

The industry trend toward higher-capacity cars continued with boxcars in the 1990s, as manufacturers began building — and railroads began buying — excess-height, 110-ton capacity 50- and 60-foot cars. Built by Gunderson, Johnstown America, Trinity, NSC, and others, these cars have double plug doors, reinforced floors, and an inside height allowing two layers of wide paper rolls stacked on end. Most Class I railroads acquired these cars, along with many private owners.

Trailer Train began buying fleets of these cars for pool service, featuring the same basic paint scheme and operational goals of earlier Railbox cars. The FBOX cars are 50 feet long, excess height (Plate F, 13'-1" interior height) cars with a single 10- or 12-foot plug-door car. The TBOX cars are similar, but 60 feet long with double plug doors. Both versions can often be found in paper service.

Car selection can depend on dock, trackage, and structure clearance restrictions at the shipper and receiver. The 60-foot cars, although they have become the new industry standard, have posed problems for some shippers in this regard.

BOXCAR QUALITY CLASSIFICATIONS

Boxcars are continually evaluated and graded for their condition. They are classified A, B, or C (with a couple of additional variations), with Class A the highest-quality car. Cars (other than Class W) may shift among classifications — for example, a Class B or C car can be upgraded and repaired to become a Class A car.

These classifications are generally not labeled on the car exterior. An exception was Canadian National, which for several years marked boxcars with a yellow circle with letter grade on the lower side of its boxcars (below).

In the early 1960s, Canadian National began posting boxcar quality grades on car exteriors with replaceable yellow disks or painted circles and letters. Canadian National

	ROOF	LINING/ WALLS	FLOOR	DOORS
Class A	Watertight	Intact and smooth, no splinters or protruding nails or fasteners; watertight	No leaks, no odor, no oil spots or stains, no contamination	Watertight fixtures, including locks and hasps
Class B	Watertight	Intact, watertight	Won't leak lading. No protruding patches, no leaks, no odor, no contamination	Watertight fixtures, including locks and hasps
Class C	Not watertight	Poor	Will hold rough freight	Fixtures, including locks and hasps, in good condition
Class K	Car is reported to have carried toxic or hazardous cargo; it must be physically inspected before reclassifying.			
Class U	Car is unfit for loading.			
Class W	Car has carried certain types of municipal hazardous or toxic waste; is considered contaminated and can only carry contaminated lading. This class assignment is permanent once assigned.			
Class X	Meets Class A criteria, but contains refuse (often scrap from unloading) and must be cleaned.			
Class Y	Meets Class B criteria, but contains refuse and must be cleaned.			
Class Z	Meets Class C criteria, but contains refuse and must be cleaned.			

Paper and pulp loading in the 2020s account for more than half of North American boxcar loads (about 52% by 2020); food products are the next-largest group, at 18%, then lumber/wood products at 16%.

Loading and unloading

The loading process varies by product type and era. For cases and cartons of finished sheet products, cases were generally loaded directly onto the car floor by hand into the 1960s. As wide-door boxcars became more common, pallets were loaded directly into the cars by forklifts or hand-pulled pallet jacks.

For paper rolls, hand trucks were often used in the steam era for loading and unloading, as the image on the bottom of page 56 shows. This required great care, especially for taller and heavier rolls, to guard against damage to the roll ends from leaning, tipping, or dropping them quickly. Finished rolls usually weigh at least 1,000 pounds, and some can exceed 5,000 pounds, so not only are they easily damaged — they can cause great harm and damage themselves if mishandled or if they shift in transit.

Most mills turned to modified loaders on forklifts by the 1940s. These have curved arms that clamp to the roll, allowing careful, precise placement of rolls. They're the only real option when stacking one roll atop another.

Loading patterns in boxcars vary by roll size (diameter and roll width) and car length, interior height, and weight capacity. Rolls are generally placed all the way to each end of a car, with additional rolls added against the first ones to keep rolls from shifting. Any gap in the middle (at the doorway) is filled; on modern cars, this is done with disposable airbags (called disposable inflatable dunnage, or DID, bags).

If a partial second layer is added, this will be at each end, with abutting rolls on the lower level placed on risers to help block the upper-level rolls in position.

CHAPTER SIX

PULPWOOD CARS

Hauling pulpwood from cutting areas to paper mills was the job of railroads for short- and medium-haul distances through the 1960s. Railroads accomplished this with cars of many designs, including purpose-built bulkhead flat cars, cars rebuilt from old flatcars and boxcars, and gondolas and even boxcars.

Norfolk Southern bulkhead-style pulpwood racks of different designs trail a pair of the railroad's Baldwin road switchers in the early 1970s. The flatcar-type cars were the most common pulpwood carriers. They were economical but suffered from challenges including speed restrictions, loads shifting, and logs falling off of cars. *Trains* Magazine collection

As Chapter 4 explained, trucks captured more and more of this traffic by the 2000s and now carry most of it, although some railroads still get occasional loads (only about 4,000 loads per year as of 2020).

Car types and classes

Dedicated pulpwood cars, regardless of specific type (flat, gondola, dump) are designated as a specific car type: AAR class LP (as opposed to standard flatcars, which are class F). The definition of an LP car is "… an open-top car having a solid bottom and fixed ends, with or without fixed sides (either slatted or solid). Suitable for hauling pulpwood." In addition, listings in the *Official Railway Equipment Register* (ORER) through the 1970s usually include a "pulp" notation in the notes column for each railroad's cars.

The styles of cars used varied greatly by railroad and region. Railroads in the Southeast and Northeast tended to opt for flatcar-style pulpwood cars (pulp racks) almost exclusively. In the Midwest and West, standard or converted gondolas were typically the car of choice.

The Southern Railway, as an example, carried a lot of pulpwood and had the largest U.S. pulpwood car fleet: about 6,400 rack cars as of 1962 (and still about 3,800 by 1981). The Milwaukee Road carried a lot of pulpwood to mills in northern Wisconsin and Michigan's Upper Peninsula. The Milwaukee, on the other hand, relied primarily on gondolas. Some of these were older modified cars, but the railroad relied heavily on standard (GS) gons instead of dedicated cars.

We'll look at car details in a bit, but obtaining an ORER for the period you model can be a huge help in figuring out what cars (and car types) railroads had in service during specific years.

Because pulpwood is a relatively low-value lading, and hauls are generally short, many railroads actually lost money by hauling it — they did it to retain the more lucrative traffic in finished paper. This means railroads historically avoided investing in expensive equipment to carry pulpwood. Many railroads rebuilt older, obsolete freight cars into pulpwood cars — notable examples are large groups of Southern's fleet that have been rebuilt from retired boxcars.

Let's take a look at the different car types and styles that have carried pulpwood.

Through the 1920s, boxcars were the most common way to transport pulpwood. Loading and unloading were strictly done manually. Some areas continued the practice into the 1940s and later — this scene is from 1943 in San Augustine, Texas. John Vachon, Library of Congress

Boxcars

Into the 1930s, boxcars were the most common way of moving pulpwood. Railroads loved this, as boxcars were the most common car type, railroads didn't have to make any additional investments in equipment, and older and lower-grade (Class C, explained in Chapter 5) cars were fine for pulpwood service. Loading and unloading were done by hand, and although it was a tedious, cumbersome work, labor was still cheap and the volume of traffic at any given location or mill was relatively small.

Workers would hand-stack logs ("bolts"), transferring them directly from a truck or wagon or from a trackside stockpile. Logs were stacked in rows across the car, starting at each end, and at the doorway additional logs were placed between the stacks to keep them from shifting. Unloading at the mill was likewise done by hand, as Chapter 3 showed.

With the increase in mechanized log handling and the resulting higher volumes of traffic, more efficient methods and different cars soon appeared. However, some boxcar loading continued in the 1940s and even into the 1950s.

Flatcars

Flatcars provide the easiest access and offer flexibility in that they can be loaded and unloaded either by hand or mechanically. A pulpwood flat, however, is different than a standard bulkhead flatcar. The primary difference is that both sides of the deck slope inward (at about a 10-degree

PULPWOOD CAR MODELS

In HO, pulpwood racks have been offered by Atlas (a SIECO prototype and an older 42-foot car), Walthers (including a 63-foot side-stake car), Athearn, and Con-Cor. In N, cars have been made by Atlas and N Scale Kits (the Magor 64-foot, center-bulkhead car).

Molded pulpwood loads have been made by Chooch, Atlas, and Walthers, and some smaller companies have produced plaster and resin loads for specific model cars. Loads can also be made from real branches and twigs. These can be glued directly to a car, or made as a removable load (see Chapter 10 for tips on sealing wood).

angle) in a shallow V shape, meeting in a channel running longitudinally down the center of the deck. They are often called "V-deck" cars.

This design allows stacking parallel rows of 4- to 5-foot logs along each side of the car. Each stack angles inward, stabilizing the loads and minimizing the chances of the stacks shifting outward during train movement. No additional side restraints are used.

A bulkhead at each end holds the ends of the stacks in place. Many cars have a vertical line marked on the interior wall of each bulkhead to give workers a guideline in keeping the stacks even. Some included markings at the top of the bulkhead to indicate the top level of logs, helping ensure cars didn't exceed their weight limit. Bulkhead heights ranged from 5 to 7 feet above the deck on early cars and up to 9 feet for longer 70-ton cars (this varied by the cars' load limits and length between bulkheads).

Depending upon the width of the deck and the length of the logs (depending upon mill specifications and railroad clearance, they were usually cut to 4'-0" to 5'-0" lengths),

Pulpwood cars with four- and eight-foot bolts await picking up by a Maine Central local freight in 1979. Note how the load in the near car has shifted, and is bowing outward to the right. William Metzger

The Southern Railway converted hundreds of older boxcars to pulpwood racks, including 300 cars in the 126000 series in 1953. The V-shaped deck is apparent in this view. Southern Ry.

Delaware & Hudson 8002 is an example of a General Steel Castings 38-foot cast car kit. It was built by Chesapeake & Ohio in 1956 and acquired by D&H in 1959. Note the grated V-shaped deck and the loading guide markings on the inside of the bulkhead. Delaware & Hudson

This 70-ton car, built by ACF for Louisville & Nashville, features all-welded construction with a straight channel-style side sill. The V-deck is visible at the end below the bulkhead. The inside length is 41'-5", deck width is 9'-2", and the height to the top of the bulkheads is 12'-5". Louisville & Nashville

Greenville built a series of 500 pulpwood racks for Southern in 1973 (140000 series). The 80-ton cars were 50 feet long with a bulkhead height above deck of 9'-2" and a width of 9'-4". Southern Ry.

the logs' ends were either within the side sill/bulkhead width, or had a specific allowed amount of overhang. Stenciling on the Southern car above indicates overhang beyond each side sill may not exceed 10 inches.

Loaded cars presented operational challenges. Logs often shifted because of slack action or "rock-and-roll" motion of trains, and logs could fall from cars (sometimes dramatically with significant distance when slack ran in or out or a car rocked suddenly). The high-angle view on page 67 shows a load that has begun to shift. If you model a stretch of railroad that hosts significant pulpwood traffic in these cars, a realistic touch is to include scattered pulpwood logs along the ballast shoulder and right of way. (Workers quickly learned not to spend time next to the cars, especially when they were in motion.)

Because of this, railroads had speed restrictions for pulpwood racks when loaded, often limiting them to 25 to 30 mph (and thus usually keeping them in local or way freights). Railroads also sometimes called for restricted speeds when trains with pulpwood loads met other trains or when other trains passed these cars.

These speed restrictions generally didn't severely impact operations, as hauls were usually not long, and often took place on slow-speed branches that served pulpwood loadouts and mills. They could, however, be a thorn in a dispatcher's side when in mainline freight trains.

In spite of their shortcomings, these cars were economical to build and use, and they became the most-common pulpwood car through the 1970s. Along with railroads' home-built cars, manufacturers building them new included ACF, Bethlehem, Magor, General Steel Castings (GSC), Greenville, Pullman-Standard, Southern Iron & Equipment Co. (SIECO), and Thrall.

As noted, the Southern was the largest user of these cars, first converting about 500 of them from 40-foot flatcars from 1934-1937. Next came the largest group, 2,710 cars converted from old 36-foot wood boxcars from 1940 to 1951, then 900 more from old 40-foot double-sheathed furniture boxcars, done in 1953. These had boxy ends (bulkheads), with the steel cut-down old boxcar ends. New cars were also added to the fleet over the years.

Other railroads operating large numbers of flatcar-style racks (with 1962 roster totals in parentheses) included Atlantic Coast Line (3,800); Bangor & Aroostook (630); Central of Georgia (1,560); Gulf, Mobile & Ohio (1,180); Illinois Central (2,050); Louisville & Nashville (1,380); Maine Central (494); Missouri Pacific (1,200); and Seaboard Air Line (3,260).

These may not seem like big numbers, especially considering fleets of other car types, but keep in mind that some of these were small railroads. For example, the Maine Central's pulpwood cars represented 15% of its total car fleet.

Car size is rated by weight capacity and cord capacity, as well as inside length (IL, measured between bulkhead walls) and inside height (IH, measured from the deck surface to the top of the bulkhead). Sizes grew larger, from 20- to 30-cord capacity of older 50-ton cars with an IL from 32 to 42 feet, to to 37 cords for newer, longer (up to 50-foot) 70- and 100-ton versions.

Kansas City Southern had a series of 300 long, heavy-duty pulpwood cars. The 65-foot cars had a 57'-3" inside length and a 115-ton capacity. Several of them head to a Shreveport, La., mill in 1977. Jim Hediger

Magor built long (64-foot inside length) welded-construction pulpwood racks for Bangor & Aroostook (shown) and Maine Central in 1964. The cars had a center partition to stabilize the load. A loaded car rolls behind a BL2 (at right) in 1965. J. David Ingles

Car designs and details varied widely among manufacturers, and often between orders and railroads. To identify cars, look for the construction method (welded, riveted, or cast); side sill style (straight or fishbelly) and depth; deck style (smooth or corrugated and with or without drain holes down the center); brake gear (and brake wheel type and location); and the style (design) and height of the bulkheads.

A notable variation came from General Steel Castings (GSC), which in the 1950s provided kits to several railroads for pulpwood versions of its popular cast-steel flatcars. These were distinctive, with a double-taper fishbelly side sill. They were made in two versions, initially with a 38-foot IL and a later 45-foot version.

By the time 100-ton freight cars became standard in the early 1960s, pulpwood traffic was declining rapidly.

The 1980s and later saw a shift toward long (even tree-length) logs for pulpwood, carried longitudinally on flatcars with vertical side stakes. This 70-foot (IL) Escanaba & Lake Superior log car in 1996 includes markings for load limits for hardwood and softwood logs. The paired vertical stakes allow loaders to grab logs between them. J. David Ingles

This Wisconsin Central side-stake car in 2005 shows how aligning logs with the wide gaps in the stakes allows mechanical claw-style loaders to pick the logs from the car. The WC made 75 Mega Log Haulers in 2001 by semipermanently coupling pairs of 50-foot bulkhead cars together. J. David Ingles

Few traditional-style 100-ton pulpwood rack cars were built new, but a distinctive version built by Magor for Bangor & Aroostook and Maine Central was a 100-ton, 72-foot car that included an intermediate bulkhead in the center of the car to help stabilize the load — otherwise a challenge on longer cars.

The 1970s and later saw a shift in some areas to long (65-foot) flatcars that carry longer logs longitudinally, using tall stakes on the sides to hold loads in place. These cars offer several advantages. Operationally they're more stable, keeping the load firmly in place with no lateral shifting as with V-deck cars. This allowed removing or increasing speed limits for pulp cars. They were more easily (and economically) worked by mechanical claw-style loaders, speeding loading and unloading and allowing more control compared to traditional cars. A change for some of these cars is their AAR classification, which became FL (indicating a log car) instead of LP for pulpwood service.

Some of these cars were built with side stakes that could be folded down; most of these were later fixed or welded in place, as operators found there was little need for the feature.

Another option done by some railroads by request of paper mills was carrying longer (8- to 10-foot) logs on standard bulkhead cars. The result was a more stable load; conventional bulkhead cars could be used, as the V-deck was then not needed.

Gondolas

Railroads across the Midwest and many in the Northwest tended to favor gondolas instead of bulkhead V-deck cars for pulpwood. Advantages included a readily available supply of cars that didn't require special equipment, with loads that tended to be more stable — although part of the load extended above the car sides, the sides provided the bottoms of the stacks with a solid base of support. These could be mill or GS (general-service) cars, including drop-bottom cars.

Railroads carrying significant pulpwood traffic in gondolas included Algoma Central, Burlington Northern, Canadian National, Chicago & North Western, Great Northern, Milwaukee Road, Northern Pacific, and Soo Line. In addition, some paper companies owned their own cars.

Thrall built these 61-foot non-bulkhead log racks for Missouri Pacific subsidiary Chicago & Eastern Illinois in the 1970s. They're in operation in 2000 for new owner Camas Prairie RailNet, bringing pulpwood to the large tissue-paper mill at Lewiston, Idaho (in the background). J. David Ingles

Some of these railroads converted older gondolas to pulpwood service; these received the LP classification. This conversion could involve removing the side sheeting between posts (see the Milwaukee Road cars on pages 73 and 74), adding permanent end posts, and adding extended side posts for longitudinal loading.

The usual method of loading a standard gon was to stand several logs on end at each end to serve as bulkheads. Logs were then loaded laterally in the car in the same way as with a flatcar.

Gons carrying pulpwood faced speed restrictions as with standard pulpwood racks. Also, safety measures were required when cars were routed over multiple-track territory. In particular, wire mesh was specified in AAR loading guidelines starting in 1974 (visible in photo of the Algoma Central gon on page 75). The mesh extended to the top of the load, with stakes supporting it (rules required that the stakes be located close enough together "to prevent any portion of load from moving beyond sides of the car"). Nails, screws, and staples were not allowed for attaching wire mesh.

Midwestern railroads favored gondolas for pulpwood. This Northern Pacific GS gon has logs stacked vertically at each end to serve as bulkheads. The car, built in 1940, is shown in 1974. *Trains* Magazine collection

Decline

Pulpwood log traffic dropped significantly from the 1980s onward, and few if any new pulpwood cars were built after the 1970s. Trucks are large and efficient, and a semi can haul multiple loads each day, compared to a railcar that takes several days to complete a single cycle. Together with the low revenue and value of the loads, railroads didn't fight to keep the traffic. In 2019, just 12,000 pulpwood loads were carried by North American railroads.

Magor's side-dump pulpwood cars were used briefly by Bangor & Aroostook. A hydraulic mechanism raised the track to tilt the car, dumping bolts into a pond at the paper mill at North Twin (Millinocket), Maine. Cars had to be switched one at a time and uncoupled on the dump track. Bangor & Aroostook

SIDE-DUMP CAR

A unique solution to the challenges of efficiently carrying pulpwood bolts was a side-dump gondola-style car built in 1946 by Magor for Bangor & Aroostook. These 50-ton cars (originally Nos. 5000-5099; later renumbered 1-199) were 48 feet long (inside length of 46 feet) and divided into two compartments. The sides were hinged at the top — one section for each compartment.

The cars were loaded through the open top and unloaded on a specially equipped track. Cars had to be unloaded one at a time, so had to be uncoupled and spotted over the dumper, which the mill did with a small industrial locomotive. The car was clamped in place by locking bars that attached to lugs on the bottom sides of the car. A hydraulic cylinder actuated the car side doors, unlatching them, and the track under each truck hydraulically tilted to unload the car. As the gates swung open, the logs were released, sliding down the incline into the mill pond. The slope of the incline was about 27 degrees.

Each swinging side door had a small (4'-6" wide) sliding door. These could be used to unload the car manually if necessary. Each car had a light weight of 56,000 pounds and a capacity of 113,000 pounds.

Although a fascinating solution, the cars did not last long in service. It was simply too much special equipment and too many operational moves to be practical for a low-value product.

The Milwaukee Road served several paper mills on its Valley Line in northern Wisconsin at the time of this 1974 photo. The MILW gon at right has been modified by having side panels removed; standard Northern Pacific and Great Northern GS gondolas follow. Stan Mailer

This 1976 view shows several Milwaukee Road gons loaded with pulpwood logs. The gons at left have been modified with permanent bulkheads and steel side stakes to carry logs longitudinally. Stan Mailer

Workers load a composite-side Chicago & North Western gondola with 8-foot bolts using a crane with hooks and chains. The process was laborious and dangerous. Keith Kohlmann collection

Two Milwaukee Road gons carry full loads of pulpwood in 1972. The cars have been lightened by cutting away the side panels behind the exterior bracing. Note the PULPWOOD LOADING ONLY stenciling. Keith Kohlmann collection

Several Soo Line and Milwaukee Road gondolas loaded with eight-foot bolts await a local freight in this early 1990s scene. Note the angled logs serving as bulkheads at each end. Jim Hediger

An Algoma Central gondola carries a load of debarked pulpwood logs in 1964. The wire mesh around the top portion of the load was mandated in some situations and routes by AAR rules. John Ingles; Jeff Wilson collection

CHAPTER SEVEN

WOOD CHIP CARS

The market for chips as a source for pulp began developing in the 1940s. It began with grinding the scrap wood from cutting lumber, screening it, and transporting the resulting chips to mills as raw material for paper. This later expanded to facilities grinding entire logs and trees remotely and shipping the chips instead of logs (see Chapter 4).

This car, one of a 200-car order built by Thrall for Northern Pacific in 1966, was among the first high-capacity all-steel chip cars. It has a 100-ton, 6,000-cubic-foot capacity. The 60-foot car has a 14'-3" height, shorter than later excess-height cars. Thrall's cars have heavy, tapered side posts that meet underbody cross members. John Ingles; Jeff Wilson collection

This late start meant that railroads — which had tens of thousands of pulpwood cars by the 1950s — didn't have any specialized cars for carrying chips. However, as the market for wood chips grew, railroads quickly adapted, progressing from home-modified cars to big purpose-built cars that were eventually among the largest cars on the rails.

Like pulpwood, wood chips were generally a low-revenue commodity for railroads, but carrying chips helped the railroads serving mills to secure the more-valuable traffic in finished paper products. They could be found on almost any railroad that served paper and lumber mills.

Let's take a look at the evolution of wood chip cars.

Converted cars

In theory, just about any open-top gondola or hopper can be used to carry wood chips. However, chips are extremely light compared to other bulk products that ride in open cars (such as coal or crushed rock). Chips weigh only 20 to 25 pounds per cubic foot (cf) — as a comparison, lump coal weighs about 50 pounds/cf.

This means a full load of wood chips by volume in a standard-size gon or hopper will be well under the car's weight limit, making it an economic loss to transport in large quantities.

Railroads first solved this by modifying existing cars — usually older hopper cars and gondolas — by adding side and end extensions that increased interior capacity. A primary consideration was how the cars were to be unloaded at the paper mill. Some preferred bottom-dump cars, so hopper cars were the starting point; others used a clamshell crane or tractor-mounted loader to unload cars, so preferred gondolas.

Cars were modified in many ways, with each style unique to the railroad doing the work. Steel extensions were often welded to the tops of gondolas or hoppers. These could have external or internal support posts, usually done

Most early chip cars were converted hoppers. The Boston & Maine welded steel-plate extensions atop a three-bay, offset-side hopper to create this 4,700-cf version. It's at Woodsville, N.H., in May 1966. Dwight A. Smith

Canadian National in 1970 rebuilt 300 three-bay, offset-side hopper cars with side extensions, extending the height to 15'-2" and giving them a 4,488-cf capacity. John Ingles; Jeff Wilson collection

to match the car. Others used wood planks or plywood for extensions.

Overall car height varied based on clearances on the routes involved. Many of these cars were assigned to specific mills and traveled on dedicated routes between the lumber mill or loadout facility and paper mill.

Railroads modifying cars included Boston & Maine; Canadian National; Canadian Pacific; Chesapeake & Ohio; Louisville & Nashville; Grand Trunk Western; Gulf, Mobile & Ohio; Milwaukee Road; Missouri Pacific; Norfolk Southern; Northern Pacific; Pacific Great Eastern; St. Louis-San Francisco; Southern; Southern Pacific; Spokane, Portland & Seattle; Western Maryland; and Western Pacific. Tracking exact numbers and rosters can be difficult, but many include notations in their *Official Railway Equipment Register* entries specifying wood chip service, and their exterior heights will also be listed in the entries.

Most of these were 50-ton cars with a resulting cubic capacity around 4,500 cf. Later in the 1950s and into the 1960s, some railroads modified 70-ton cars. These were often longer, resulting in capacities topping 5,000 cf.

Although these cars solved the initial challenge of getting chips from the source to the mill, they were far from ideal. They were often economical to build, but older equipment was not as reliable as new cars. The modified cars were also heavy — they were originally built to carry coal and other denser products, and had sides and bracing

In the early 1960s, Gulf, Mobile & Ohio converted about 300 two-bay, exterior-post hoppers into wood chip cars. The cars were rebuilt with continuous posts and side sheets. The cars stood 15'-6" tall — making them early excess-height cars — for a 3,500-cf capacity. Number 82296 is shown just after rebuilding in 1962. John Ingles; Jeff Wilson collection

Northern Pacific converted many old 41-foot drop-bottom GS gons to wood chip service by adding wood side extensions with planks (as here) or plywood. Exact dimensions varied among cars, but most were about 15'-2" tall with capacities around 4,000 cf. Some operated into the late 1960s. *Trains* magazine collection

This Canadian Pacific car is an example of a mill gondola converted to a chip car with side extensions. The 57-foot car has an end door (on the far end). It stands 14'-10" tall and has a 5,500-cf capacity. It was still in service — riding on solid-bearing trucks — in 1995. J. David Ingles

Some railroads converted old boxcars into wood chip gondolas. Apache built 50 cars in this manner in 1972, splicing two steel boxcars, plating over the door openings, and removing the roof. The resulting 60-foot, 5800-cf car is used in rotary-dump service. It's shown in June 1973. Jeff Wilson collection

The Louisiana & North West served many lumber and paper customers. This L&NW boxcar has a paper door — typically used for bulk grain service — for carrying wood chips. The X29-design car was built in 1929 and is carrying chips in June 1961. John Ingles; Jeff Wilson collection

AAR CLASSES FOR CHIP CARS

Through the 1960s the AAR designation for chip cars was initially LP, the same as with pulpwood cars. This caused some confusion (and can make it difficult to identify cars by listings in the *Official Railway Equipment Register*). By the late 1970s, however, hopper-style wood chip cars were usually classified HTS (HT is an open-top, self-clearing car with three or more transverse hoppers; the "S" is for special service) and gons were GTS (GT is an open-top car with fixed sides, solid bottom, and fixed or hinged ends; "S" for special service).

that was overkill for the less-dense chip loads. In spite of this, some would remain in service well into the era of purpose-built 100-ton cars, albeit often on secondary or short-haul routes, or to cover periods of heavy traffic.

Another method of modifying cars was removing the roofs from boxcars and sealing the side door openings to create tall gondolas. On these, the sides were often extended upward; some railroads lengthened the cars as well. Railroads doing this included Apache; Bangor & Aroostook; CN; CP; Central of Georgia; Great Northern; Maine Central; Milwaukee Road; Northern Pacific; and Southern.

Yet another solution was to use standard boxcars, but with temporary removable doors in the openings (like paper grain doors). Among railroads doing this were Chicago & North Western; Dakota, Minnesota & Eastern; Louisiana & North West; Soo Line; and Wisconsin Central. Some railroads permanently modified these cars by removing the sliding side doors (saving tare weight). This was the least-expensive option, but didn't allow as much capacity as other cars. A few of these operations lasted into the 2000s, notably on the DM&E and WC. Mills using these cars generally unloaded them pneumatically (by vacuum).

Standard car capacity moved to 70 tons and then 100 tons by the early 1960s. In 1963 the AAR approved 100-ton cars for unrestricted interchange, with a gross rail load (total weight — the load and the car itself) of 263,000 pounds, and at the same time increased the GRL for 70-ton cars from 210,000 to 220,000 pounds.

This meant that the rebuilt and modified cars were simply undersized for the job they had to do. That, together with the increasing volume of chip traffic, meant that railroads and car builders needed to develop better ways of carrying chips efficiently.

Purpose-built cars

New cars built specifically to carry wood chips began appearing in 1957. These eventually followed two basic styles: bottom-dump hoppers (with transverse bays, like coal hoppers) and gondolas, usually with end doors. There are exceptions, but for the most part railroads and mills in the East and Southeast prefer hoppers, while those in the Northwest opt for gondolas. Part of the reason for this is the weather. In colder climates, wood chips can become wet and freeze in the cars, meaning they don't always flow well through cars' bottom outlet gates. The ultimate choice is by the specific mill receiving the chips, tied to the unloading processes used.

Regardless of the style, purpose-built chip cars share similar characteristics. The first is size: The cubic capacity reflects a full load of chips that will "cube out" to match the car's weight capacity (70 or 100 tons). These cars are longer than their coal-carrying brothers, and — especially for 100-ton versions — many are built to excess-height (high-cube) dimensions.

Wood chip carbodies also have lighter side construction compared to coal cars, although this often isn't evident in simple viewing. Although many have heavy visible external bracing, the side walls and panels are generally thinner, resulting in lighter car weight (enabling larger payloads).

Southern's 6,800-cf side-door chip cars, built in 1960, carried significantly more chips than a standard hopper car. They were emptied by a mechanical "sweeper" reaching into the side. Southern Railway

SOUTHERN'S SIDE-DUMP CARS

The Southern Railway designed these gondola-style, 70-ton wood chip cars with lower-side doors that lifted upward to discharge the load. The car shown, No. 130583, was built in April 1960 as one of a series of 100 cars (130500-130599). The car has 6,800-cf capacity, a 54-foot inside length, and stands 16'-3" tall, making it among the first excess-height chip cars. Southern's promotional material at the time bragged that a single one of these cars carried 2½ times as many chips of a conventional 70-ton hopper.

After the side doors are lifted, a mechanical "raker" sweeps the chips out of the car and into a below-track conveyor. The railroad eventually acquired about 400 similar cars across five series, which were given AAR designation GD (gondola with side doors). Mechanical issues led to the side doors being closed permanently, and the cars were then operated as standard wood chip gons. They were redesignated LP in the 1960s.

Here's a look at the details of several types of wood chip cars that have been built.

Gondola-style cars

Railroads buying new gondola-style cars were primarily in the western U.S. and Canada, including Canadian National; Great Northern; Milwaukee Road, Northern Pacific; Pacific Great Eastern; Southern Pacific; Spokane, Portland & Seattle; and Union Pacific; later owners of these cars included BC Rail; Burlington Northern; Montana Rail Link; and Golden West Service. The Southern Railway also owned some gondola chip cars among its large fleet of hoppers.

The first purpose-built wood chip cars were 500 gondolas built by General American for Southern Pacific in 1957. The 70-ton steel cars had alternating heavy and light vertical posts, a 52'-11" inside length, 4,590-cf interior, and — unlike later 100-ton cars — were not excess height. Also unlike later cars, they had drop bottoms (in a style like earlier general-service gons, not transverse bays like hoppers).

Soo Line rebuilt several 50-foot boxcars, removing their sliding doors (thus saving several hundred pounds of tare weight) and using paper doors reinforced with wood strips to carry chips. Stencils include "WOOD CHIP LOADING ONLY" and "MISSING DOOR STANDARD TO CAR." This car is shown just after conversion in 1986. Jeff Wilson collection

Among the first purpose-built chip cars were 500 drop-bottom, all-steel cars built by General American for Southern Pacific in 1957. The 70-ton cars (railroad class G-70-15) originally had alternating heavy/light vertical side posts (top). In the late 1960s, many cars were rebuilt with composite sides, receiving plywood sheathing inside combination vertical and angled posts (bottom), becoming class G-70-15A. Both cars are shown in 1969. Two photos: John Ingles; Jeff Wilson collection

The cars, originally railroad class G-70-15, were rebuilt by SP starting in 1966 with plywood sides and new side bracing with heavy vertical and diagonal posts, giving them a distinct appearance compared to the originals (see the photos at left). The rebuilt cars were reclassed G-70-15A. Not all were rebuilt; all were off the roster by 1986.

The SP also received the first excess-height gons, 200 composite-side 60-foot cars with a 7,466-cf capacity, from Pullman-Standard in mid-1965. Unlike the earlier cars, they had no bottom doors, and were designed for rotary-dump only.

Southern in 1960 experimented with gondola-style cars with side doors for dumping (see "Southern side-dump cars" on page 79). The 70-ton cars had a 6,800-cf capacity.

Gunderson in 1965 delivered the first order of 100-ton composite-side cars to GN (50 cars, initially assigned to St. Regis Paper mill at Tacoma) and SP&S (70 cars). The 6,123-cf cars had heavy vertical and diagonal side beams forming a truss, and — unusual for the period — ¾" plywood for the interior sheathing. They had single end doors. Gunderson followed with another order of composite cars to GN in 1966, followed by all-steel versions.

These and successive gons were emptied at mills either by rotary dumping, by tipping them on end (cars had doors on one or both ends), by clamshell unloading cranes, by vacuum unloading (through the top), or by front-end loaders that entered through the end door.

Similar composite and all-steel cars were soon being built by Gunderson, FMC, Magor, National Steel Car, Pacific Car & Foundry, Pullman-Standard, and Thrall. (Gunderson — Gunderson Brothers Engineering Co., or GBEC — became a division of FMC in 1965, after which production is often labeled as FMC-GBEC.)

Spotting features include the overall size, including length, height, and cubic capacity (which would grow to 7,400 cf by 1980), side framing (number and style of vertical posts; number, placement, and style of horizontal braces), underbody cross members,

Burlington Northern No. 585414 carries a chip load through Portland, Ore., in the mid-1990s. Built in 1966, it's from the second batch of composite-side cars built by Gunderson for Great Northern. The distinctive 100-ton cars have a 6,048-cf capacity. Jeff Wilson

This Montana Rail Link car was built by FMC for Burlington Northern in 1972. FMC cars have vertical posts thinner in style than other builders, with uniform thickness; horizontal members are slightly thinner. The 100-ton car has a 6,810-cf interior. Jeff Wilson

number of end doors, and end and end door designs.

Thrall and later Gunderson cars had heavy vertical members connecting to heavy underbody crossmembers. FMC cars had shallow vertical posts (significantly lighter than other cars) with a distinctive pattern of horizontal braces between some vertical members.

Smooth-side (internal-post) cars were built in the mid-1970s by FMC, and PC&F built large (7,400-cf) internal-post cars for SP in 1979. The FMC cars have a visible horizontal seam line that the PC&F cars lack.

Among the last chip gons were two series (275 total cars) of 7,526-cf cars built in the early 1980s by Ortner for Southern: 68-foot cars, 16 feet tall, with heavy vertical external posts.

The largest wood chip cars were bathtub-style cars built by Johnstown America for Norfolk Southern and Federal Paperboard (reporting marks FPBX; owned by International Paper). These had 8,253-cf interiors, were 67 feet long (63'-7" inside length), and featured a design similar to the company's popular BethGon coal gondolas, with "tubs" that extended down from the floor between the trucks.

Hoppers

Hopper-style wood chip cars were favored by railroads in the Southeast, with major owners including Atlantic Coast Line, Louisville & Nashville, Seaboard Air Line, Southern, and later (through mergers) CSX, Norfolk Southern, and Seaboard Coast Line.

Among the first were a series of 400 cars built in 1959 for Atlantic Coast Line. The 70-ton cars had a 5,400-cf capacity and embossed side panels. This would become common on chip hopper cars, done to increase strength on the thin side panels.

Greenville built a series of 200 wood chip hoppers for Seaboard Air Line in 1962. The 70-ton cars had a capacity of 5,850 cf and had longitudinal doors (in the manner of ballast cars). Greenville followed the next year with another order of cars but with cross-mounted doors, including similar cars for Central of Georgia and L&N.

The primary builders of wood chip hoppers were Greenville, Magor, and Ortner. Spotting features include the overall size (length and height), number and style of outlet bays, number of vertical posts, panel styles (plain or embossed in various patterns), and details such as ladders and end design.

As with gondolas, hoppers quickly grew larger with the move to 100-ton cars after 1963. Chip cars would eventually stretch to 70 feet in length, stand 16'-2" above the rails, and have capacities of 7,500 cf and larger.

Among the last hopper-style chip cars built were an order built by Greenville for the Southern in 1980: cars with a 7,526-cf capacity and 68'-7" inside length.

Demise

Wood chip traffic dropped significantly from the 1970s onward, although the commodity hasn't vanished entirely: in 2019, just over 40,000 chip loads were carried by rail. However, few new chip cars have been built since the early 1980s. Many older cars were retired through the 1990s, with others sold by original owners to leasing companies (or paper companies).

MODELING

In HO scale, Walthers has offered models of Thrall gondolas and Greenville hopper-style chip cars. InterMountain has FMC exterior- and smooth-side gondolas; ExactRail made a Gunderson 7,466-cf composite gon; and Kaslo Shops has made several gons based on BC Rail and CN prototypes. Bowser has also made a CN gon as well as a converted CN hopper car with extensions. Although long out of production, LBF offered the jumbo JohnstownAmerica cars.

In N scale, DeLuxe Innovations offered models of smooth-side and shallow- and deep-rib wood chip gondolas. CS Models has a model of an exterior-post BC Rail (Squamish-built) car.

This Canadian National car is one of a series of 300 built at its Transcona shops in 1982 (878000 series). The 6,700-cf cars have a distinctive post style and pattern, with pairs of tightly spaced posts over each truck. J. David Ingles

Thrall built this 6,740-cf chip gondola for Weyerhaeuser-owned Columbia & Cowlitz (Washington); it's shown in 1990 restenciled with reporting marks for a new owner, northern Wisconsin short line Nicolet Badger Northern. J. David Ingles

As an experiment, in 1979 Canadian National added fiberglass hoods to 250 wood chip cars assigned to southern British Columbia. The railroad stated that along with eliminating the need for nets, the hoods increased capacity by 14%. The 6,600-cf car was built by NSC. Mike Chandler

Pacific Great Eastern 9702 is one of 260 chip cars built in 1966 by Vancouver Iron & Engineering. The 6,400-cf cars had heavy vertical side posts and a slab-style end door (seen at right). The car is shown in 1972. John Ingles; Jeff Wilson collection

Ortner built 150 excess-height (16'-2") wood chip gondolas for Southern in 1980. The 7,526-cf, 70-foot car has a 65'-9" inside length. Jim Hediger

A unique design from FMC was this smooth-side (interior-post) 7,406-cf chip gondola, with a horizontal seam along the upper side. Lettering of original owner Southern Pacific is showing thorugh a patch under the stencil of new owner Willamette & Pacific in this 1996 view at Summit, Ore. J. David Ingles

Most loads were covered by mesh fabric, attached to hooks along the top of the car. This was prone to tearing and damage, and required frequent replacement. Empty cars often carried the mesh bunched and tied along one inner side or end. John Ingles; Jeff Wilson collection

This four-bay wood chip hopper was built in 1959 for Seaboard Coast Line predecessor Atlantic Coast Line. It has a 5,400-cf capacity and shows the embossed side panels typical of these cars, adding strength to the thin side sheets. It's shown in 1967. Seaboard Coast Line

Among Greenville's many riveted wood chip hopper designs was this mid-1960s interior-post (smooth-side) car, built for Rock Island and others. It's smaller than most later cars, at 57 feet long and 15 feet tall, with a 5,825-cf capacity. Central Oregon & Pacific was the latest owner of this car in 1996. J. David Ingles

Georgia-Pacific bought this six-bay, 7,000-cf chip hopper from CSX. It's shown carrying a chip load in 1993. The 68-foot car has U-channel side posts, a stepped side frame, and smooth side panels. J. David Ingles

Greenville built this 7,526-cf wood chip hopper for Southern; it's shown in 1997. The 73-foot riveted car has embossed side panels. Jeff Wilson collection

Jumbo wood chip hoppers of different designs roll on a Norfolk Southern train in 1994. The NS car is ex-Southern 133237, a 7,526-cf car built in 1970 by Greenville. Note the full-height embossing compared to the later car at left. Jeff Wilson collection

CHAPTER EIGHT

TANK CAR AND COVERED HOPPER TRAFFIC

A caustic soda tank car has been spotted for unloading at a Pennsylvania mill in the 1990s. The insulated DOT111A100W1 car was built by ACF in 1971. It carries stenciling for its lading, and also has a hazmat placard bearing the UN code for caustic soda (1824) with the corrosive graphic. The tank is lined; stenciling shows the lining was applied in January 1995. Jim Hediger

Mills require a wide variety of chemicals and additives in the papermaking process. Many of these, including chlorine, hydrogen peroxide, clay slurry, titanium dioxide, and various acids are transported by tank car. Other inbound materials can include clay, starch, and lime by covered hopper and coal in open hoppers.

These railcars are distinctive, and they provide an opportunity for varied models and operations at a mill on a layout. Understanding the differences in these cars, how they've evolved, and how various products have historically been shipped will help you model the cars and simulate operations more realistically.

There's no way we can list and show all details or variations of cars, so we'll go through the most common car types and commodities carried to mills and show representative photos from several eras. We'll start with tank cars, then touch on covered hoppers and hopper cars. See "Inbound chemicals" on page 88 for a more detailed list of how specific products have been shipped over the years.

All tank cars are not alike. In fact, there are more varieties of tank cars than any other railcar because tank cars carry a wider range of commodities than any other car type. The types of cars used — and the specific products used by individual mills — have varied widely by era, and they also depend upon the products being made as well as the pulp-making process used by each mill.

Not only do tank cars carry very specific commodities, but car designs have changed significantly from the steam era through today. This includes size (from early 40- and 50-ton cars to today's 100- and 110-ton versions) as well as details such as expansion domes (eliminated by the early 1960s), separate frames (eliminated on most car types by the early 1960s), running boards, and other features.

Chlorine tank cars

Chlorine is an extremely hazardous material. It's a gas at normal atmospheric pressure, but it's shipped in liquid form in high-pressure tank cars and vessels. Paper mills used chlorine as a bleaching agent, but its use has been largely eliminated since the 1990s.

A common early method of shipping chlorine was in small pressure vessels known as "ton containers." These measured 30 x 80 inches, weighed about 1,300 pounds empty,

A common method of shipping chlorine through the 1950s was in "ton containers" on flatcars. These cars (AAR class TMU), like this ACF-built car, carried 15 containers, clamped in cradles. Each carries 2,000 pounds of liquid chlorine and weighs 3,500 pounds loaded. John Ingles; Jeff Wilson collection

Among the first chlorine tank cars was this 8,000-gallon ACF car, an ICC105A300 car built in 1940. The high-pressure car is in ACF's Shippers' Car Line leasing fleet, and leased to Mathieson Chemicals (Mathieson Alkali Works). American Car & Foundry

Chlorine cars varied widely in size through the 1960s, so low-volume customers might receive shipments in small cars like this 2,400-gallon version. The ICC105A300W car, built by General American in 1959, is shown in 1970 leased to Michigan Chemical Corp. It wears old-style "Dangerous" placards, and obscured by grime on the upper right is a "LIQUID CHLORINE ONLY" stencil. John Ingles; Jeff Wilson collection

TANK CAR CLASSES

The thousands of commodities carried by tank car means that there are hundreds of variations in car sizes and fittings. From 1927 until 1967, the Interstate Commerce Commission (ICC) was responsible for classifying tank cars. Since that time, the Department of Transportation (DOT) took over (with Transport Canada, TC, in Canada) for cars carrying hazardous materials, with the Association of American Railroads (AAR) providing specs for cars carrying non-hazardous commodities.

The basic car classification (which is stenciled at right on each side of each car) includes initials of the appropriate governing body, then a three-digit code indicating basic car type. Additional letter codes can indicate a jacketed (J) car or one meeting post-2000 safety standards (H), with another number indicating the tank's test pressure.

Common car classes have included 103 (non-pressure with dome, common into the 1960s), 111 and 211 (non-pressure without expansion domes, standard since the early 1960s), and 105 and 112 (pressure cars). A 1980s chlorine car, for example, might be a DOT105J500W (a high-pressure — 500 psi — jacketed car).

Tank cars are further assigned car-type codes (a "T" followed by a three-digit number). There are hundreds of these, with variations indicating size, commodity, tank material, lining material, and other details. To further complicate matters, there's also the AAR mechanical designation for each car to indicate basic construction (TL is a lined tank, for example).

For extensive details on modern tank car classification, with lots of information on fittings, size, unloading details, and specific commodity requirements, see the AAR's *Field Guide to Tank Cars,* available online in PDF format at aar.org. Owner listings in various editions of the *Official Railway Equipment Register* will indicate the car code and often the classification, and some owners' listings include further details on use and assignments).

On the right side of each end, tank cars have stenciling for their class (ICC112A400W for this LPG car), plus info on the builder (ACF) and built date and safety valve information. The capacity in gallons is stenciled on the end. *Trains* Magazine collection

and could carry 2,000 pounds of liquid chlorine (hence the name). A mill could receive these by truck; they were also shipped on specialized flatcars that had racks holding 15 containers.

By the 1940s, mills more commonly received chlorine by tank car. These were insulated pressure cars (ICC type 105 — see "Tank car classes" at left), typically 4,000 to 8,000 gallons. Chlorine cars were smaller than similar LPG cars, since chlorine weighs about twice as much as LPG. As railroad weight limits increased in the 1950s and 1960s, car size increased, to 10,000 gallons or more. By the 1970s, chlorine cars were typically 17,000 to 18,000 gallons. Modern cars (since 2020) are built to DOT105H600W standards.

Through the 1960s chlorine cars often carried the logos and paint schemes of various chemical companies, including Hooker, Penn Salt, Solvay, Diamond, Wyandotte, and others. Many of these companies had the words "alkali" or "salt" in their names (since chlorine is produced by an electrical process using a salt-water solution), which sounds more friendly than "chlorine." By the 1970s, cars were usually basic black with just the owner or leasing company reporting marks.

Chlorine cars require stenciling for their lading ("CHLORINE," "LIQUID CHLORINE," or "CHLORINE LOADING ONLY") and often a warning such as "inhalation hazard." Loaded cars carry hazmat placards. These were somewhat generic into the 1970s, carrying "DANGEROUS" or "CHLORINE" lettering. Modern placards include the UN product code, which for chlorine is "1017" on a white background.

Other chemical cars

Other frequently used papermaking chemicals traveling in tank cars include sulfur, sulfuric acid, hydrogen peroxide, caustic soda (sodium hydroxide), and hydrochloric acid.

Sulfur is mined mainly in Louisiana and Texas. It was once mined and shipped in bulk dry form, but since the late 1950s the common technique to recover it is by superheating water, injecting it into below-ground (600 feet and deeper) pockets/deposits, and using compressed air to get it to the surface.

Since then, it's typically been carried in insulated, non-pressure tank cars — 17,000-gallon capacity is standard for modern 100-ton cars. The sulfur is heated to liquid form for loading and unloading. These cars often have telltale greenish-yellow spills on their sides where the product was spilled while loading and dried. Cars are stenciled "MOLTEN SULFUR" ("sulphur" is a common spelling on cars) and wear the UN code 2448.

Acid cars are specialized non-pressure tank cars that lack bottom outlets (all unloading is through valves on the top of the car), to minimize the chance of spilling corrosive or toxic products while in motion or during the unloading process.

They have specialized top-mounted control valves (under the "bonnet" cover atop the center of the car), and are typically lined with various materials to keep the specific product being carried from reacting with or etching the steel tank body.

Acid cars are stenciled with their commodity, along with information on car lining and other special equipment. Their hazmat placards reflect their loads.

Sulfuric acid (hazmat UN 1830) is the primary product of sulfur, and it is carried in non-insulated cars of 13,000 to 15,000-gallon capacity (DOT 111A100W2 specification cars).

Hydrochloric acid (hazmat UN 1789) is also carried in acid tank cars; 20,000 gallons is typical for modern 100-ton versions. Cars are rubber-lined and non-insulated.

Caustic soda (hazmat UN No. 1824) is another common product. These cars are typically around 18,000 gallons, and they are insulated with heater coils.

Hydrogen peroxide (hazmat UN 2015) requires a lined or aluminum tank. Cars are typically around 20,000 gallons and meet DOT111A100W6/7 specifications.

Kaolin and other slurries

Along with chemicals, many other additives arrive at paper mills by

This 17,300-gallon chlorine car was built by ACF in 1998. It's a typical modern chlorine carrier, a DOT105J500W car with chlorine (UN No. 1017) placard and stenciling, plus "INHALATION HAZARD") stenciling and placard. Jeff Wilson

Molten sulfur travels in non-pressure, insulated cars equipped with heating coils. The greenish-yellow sulfur sometimes spills during loading, then peels off as it cools and dries, leaving telltale blotches. This car was built in January 1981 and photographed in August 1981. J. David Ingles

Sulfuric acid is carried in uninsulated, non-pressure cars, as this one in 2005. It carries stenciling and UN 1830 placards. Sulfuric acid is heavy (about 15 pounds per gallon), so cars are relatively small — around 14,000 gallons for a modern car. Acid cars are lined, lack bottom outlets, and have special fittings on the manway atop the tank. Jeff Wilson

tank car. Since the 1970s, the typical method of shipping many powders is in slurry form, with the powder mixed with water. The resulting slurry is easier to handle than dry powder. Typical slurried products are kaolin clay, titanium dioxide, and limestone.

Tank cars for these products are general-service (non-pressure) insulated cars, AAR type 111A (or 211A) 100W1, with bottom unloading outlets and no pressure-relief valves. Size varies by the density of each product. Slope-bottom cars (both ends of the car at an angle aiming downward to the middle) are common, and enable more-efficient unloading of thick liquids. Union (UTLX) was the first to build these, with its Funnel-Flow design, but other manufacturers soon introduced their own designs.

Mills — especially those producing high-quality, coated paper — use a lot of kaolin clay, a fine, white powder mined mainly in eastern Georgia. Kaolin was originally shipped to industrial users in boxcars in 55-pound bags, then dry in bulk in covered hoppers in the 1950s. Slurry become common in the 1970s.

Clay slurry typically weighs at least 11 pounds per gallon, so tank cars carrying it are smaller than many other general-service cars, with a typical capacity is around 14,000 gallons.

A number of companies supply kaolin, and their names and logos are often prominently displayed on cars, including Englehard, Georgia Kaolin, J.M. Huber, and Thiele. Many are leased and carry the owner's reporting marks (Union, UTLX; General American, GATX; or others) with stenciling and lettering indicating the lessee. The commodity is usually stenciled on each side.

Titanium dioxide (TiO2) is also used in producing bright, glossy paper products, and it's also most often shipped as slurry in tank cars. It's heavier than kaolin slurry (about 14 pounds per gallon), so the cars involved are smaller — around 13,000 gallons — and the tanks are often smaller in diameter with a steeper bottom slope than other tank cars.

Limestone is also sometimes shipped as a slurry, in cars similar to kaolin tank cars. As with kaolin, TiO2 and limestone slurry tank cars often carry the logos and names of their companies, with commodity stenciling as well.

INBOUND CHEMICALS AND ADDITIVES AND RAILCAR TYPES

Product	How shipped
Coal (lump)	Open hopper
Fuel oil	General-purpose tank car
LPG	Pressure tank car
Sodium hydroxide (caustic soda)	Acid tank car
Sodium sulfide	Boxcar (dry in reinforced sacks or barrels)
Chlorine	Pressure tank car
Hydrogen peroxide	Specialty (aluminum) tank car
Lime	Originally sacks in boxcars; 1940s and later bulk in covered hopper; 1970s and later as slurry in tank car
Sodium carbonate (soda ash)	Covered hopper
Aluminum sulfate (granular)	Liquid solution in tank cars
Sulfur (liquid)	Insulated tank car
Sulfuric acid	Acid tank car
Titanium dioxide slurry	Tank car
Kaolin clay	Originally in bags in boxcars; 1950s and later, bulk in covered hopper; 1970s and later as slurry in tank car
Calcium magnesium carbonate (dolomite)	Dry in covered hopper
Sodium chlorate	Dry in sealed containers, or dry in aluminum covered hoppers
Into 1930s: "bleaching powder" (chlorinated lime), made by absorbing chlorine gas with nearly dry calcium hydrate (slaked lime). In the steam era, this would typically be delivered to mills in steel drums weighing 750 pounds (per a 1930 guidebook).	
As with inbound pulp logs and chips, many mills also receive these commodities via truck (in van, bulk, and tank trailers).	

Covered hoppers

Into the 1940s, materials such as clay, lime, and starch were typically bagged and shipped in standard 40-foot general-purpose boxcars. Among the first of these to travel in bulk in covered hoppers was lime (along with powdered cement) in the 1930s. These cars are short, two-bay cars (lime is a dense, heavy product), with capacities around 1,700 cubic feet for 50-ton cars through the 1950s and increasing to 3,000 cf for modern 100- and 110-ton cars.

Kaolin clay and starch are typically carried in larger, longer three-bay cars. Clay is heavier than grain, so clay cars tend to be slightly smaller than contemporary grain cars. This meant 70-ton cars of around 3,200-cf capacity by the late 1950s, growing to 4,000-cf cars with the emergence of 100-ton cars in the 1960s.

TANK CAR MODELS

Broadway Limited makes an HO 6,000-gallon pressure car for chlorine. Walthers has several HO models, including a sulfur car, general-purpose cars for fuel oil, a modern LPG car (also in N scale), and older (frame) and newer (frameless) pressure cars for chlorine. Atlas has an 11,000-gallon pressure car for LPG and modern general-service tank cars. Athearn has a 13,600-gallon acid tank car in HO and N, and in HO, a 20,000-gallon General American acid car, a modern LPG tank, a 16,000-gallon slurry car, and its older HO "chemical" tank car can pass for an early LPG or chlorine car.

In N, Micro-Trains has general-purpose tanks in older (frame with dome) and modern (frameless) styles. Bachmann has an older pressure and general-service tank.

Sunshine Models once made HO resin kits for several steam/early diesel era UTLX tank cars. Although long out of production, the kits show up online through various vendors. Also, check online for 3D-printed kits of tank cars in HO, N, and other scales. The sources vary, but you can sometimes find kits or software to print your own.

Clay and lime tend to leave residue on cars, giving them a distinctive gray, dusty appearance, often with vertical streaks (see the photos on page 92). Cars dedicated to these services are usually stenciled as such, often with additional "return to …" lettering or stenciling.

Starch likewise can travel in three-bay covered hoppers; it's also commonly carried in pressure-differential cars or General American's distinctive Airslide cars (page 93).

Soda ash and dolomite (calcium magnesium carbonate) are carried in

Cars carrying hydrochloric acid are similar to sulfuric acid cars, but larger. Built by Union Tank in 1988, this is a non-insulated 20,000-gallon car. It carries stenciling and placard (UN 1789) for HCL. It's shown in 2006. Jeff Wilson

This early caustic soda car was built by ACF in 1941 and was leased to Dow Chemical when this photo was taken in 1959. It's an insulated 8,000-gallon, ICC103W car, typical of those in caustic soda service through the 1960s. John Ingles; Jeff Wilson collection

This diminutive 4,000-gallon car, built by General American in 1948, carries hydrogen peroxide. The uninsulated, non-pressure, aluminum-tank car (ICC103A ALW) is owned by FMC/Becco. Stenciling at upper right reads "HYDROGEN PEROXIDE ONLY." John Ingles; Jeff Wilson collection

This modern non-insulated hydrogen peroxide tank car has an aluminum tank, a frame, and it has separate head shields on each end. It's shown in 2006. Jeff Wilson

the same types of covered hoppers that carry fertilizer — they generally look like grain cars, but aren't as large (about 4,000 cf for 100-ton cars and 4,250 cf for modern 110-ton cars).

Sodium chlorate, used to make chlorine dioxide on-site at mills, can be shipped in sealed containers or in aluminum covered hoppers (the material will react with steel). These are typically two-bay cars with capacities around 3,000 cf (see page 93).

All of these cars typically have individual roof hatches, as opposed to the long trough-style hatches of grain cars. Bottom outlets can be conventional (gravity), pneumatic, or combination.

Fuel

Paper mill operations require a tremendous amount of energy. The large boilers essential to operations have historically been fired by coal, fuel oil, LPG (liquified petroleum gas), or natural gas; these are supplanted by burning waste products generated during paper production. Some mills also generated their own electricity. Modern plants often have the capability to switch between fuel types based on price and availability. Regardless of the type, even a small plant may use multiple carloads of fuel per day.

Coal was the most common fuel through the 1950s. It was cheap, plentiful, and easy to transport by rail. Hopper cars of 50- or 55-ton capacity were typical through the 1950s, with

Since the 1970s, clay slurry cars have become arguably the most common tank cars found at modern paper mills. This 13,500-gallon car, built by ACF in 1978, is leased by Thiele Kaolin. It's an insulated, DOT211A100W1 car with a bottom outlet. J. David Ingles

Anglo-American Clays leases this Funnel-Flow (slope-bottom) tank car from UTLX. The car, built by Union in 1984, is a 14,000-gallon insulated DOT111A100W2 design. Kaolin cars are typically light in color and wear logos of their owners/lessees. J. David Ingles

Titanium dioxide tank cars are typically longer and lower than kaolin cars. This 11,000-gallon, non-insulated AAR 211A 100W1 car is a Funnel-Flow design with a noticeably steep tank slope. Union built this car, and it's operated by Tiona/ Millennium in 2006. Jeff Wilson

some plants accepting 70-ton cars from the 1940s onward.

Environmental regulations caused coal to fall out of favor by the 1960s, but some larger plants added upgraded emission controls to allow continued use of it. Modern plants have used 100-ton hopper cars from that period through today, generally with bottom-dump (hopper) cars unloading by gravity to between-rails pits (paper mills usually don't have the car volume to justify rotary-dump cars for coal).

Fuel oil was also commonly used. This was often heavier fuel than the common No. 2 fuel used in home heating; No. 6 ("Bunker C"), a heavy, thick oil that requires heating to flow sufficiently (and was also commonly used by oil-fired steam locomotives), was used by many mills. Its use declined through the 1960s, but some plants continued to use it as an option into the 2000s.

Fuel oil is carried in general-purpose tank cars; cars carrying Bunker C would be equipped with steam coils to enable unloading. Car sizes ranged from 8,000-10,000-gallon cars through the steam and early diesel eras, with cars to 20,000 gallons by the 1990s.

The market for LPG grew rapidly from the 1940s onward; it has a high energy content and burns much cleaner than coal or fuel oil. By the 1960s, LPG was the fuel of choice for mills in remote areas without access to natural gas pipelines.

North American built this 11,000-gallon titanium dioxide car for DuPont. Note its small diameter compared to the larger 16,000-gallon tank car at left. Stenciling is not required for TiO2, but, like kaolin, many manufacturers include lettering and logos indicating the lading on their cars. J. David Ingles

This 16,000-gallon limestone slurry car was built by ACF in 2001; it's shown in 2017 and leased to Omya, Inc. It's a slope-bottom AAR211A 100W1 car with a 110-ton capacity (286,000-pound gross rail load). Cody Grivno

From the steam era into the 1970s, fuel oil was typically delivered to mills in general-purpose tank cars like this UTLX 10,000-gallon car. Cars carrying heavy oil (like Bunker C) would be equipped with steam-heat coils. Modern frameless fuel-oil cars are larger (around 20,000 gallons). Cornelius W. Hauck

Modern LPG cars are easily spotted, as they're the largest tank cars in service. They are stenciled, and loaded cars are placarded. This 28,000-gallon, DOT112A 340W pressure car, leased by Procor to Dome Gas, was built by Union in 1973 and shown in 1976. Cars hauling LPG today are typically 33,000-gallon capacity. J. David Ingles

This 4,042-cf ACF Center Flow covered hopper is in kaolin service for the Southern Railway. Built in April 1974, the car is already weathered with clay in this photo taken two months later. The car is stenciled "FOR CLAY SERVICE ONLY." George Drury

The most common car for LPG into the 1960s was an 11,000-gallon insulated pressure car. This one was built by Union (Graver) in 1955 and leased to Tuloma Gas Products. Pressure cars (this is an ICC105A 300W) of the era lack the large expansion domes of non-pressure cars of the period. John Ingles; Jeff Wilson collection

The Sandersville Railroad is a Georgia short line known as "The Kaolin Road." This Magor-built 4,000-cf covered hopper has round roof hatches and wears the dust and streaking of its contents. Stenciling includes "FOR CLAY LOADING ONLY." Built in 1965, this car was just a year old in this 1966 photo. John Ingles; Jeff Wilson collection

This 70-ton, three-bay, 3,219-cf covered hopper is carrying Bentonite clay in this early 1970s photo. The Pullman-Standard PS-2 car is typical of those carrying clay from the late 1950s into the 1970s. It's owned by North American and leased to Federal Bentonite. Jeff Wilson collection

Soda ash can arrive at mills by covered hopper. This 4,460-cf Center Flow car, owned by FMC Chemicals, was built by ACF in May 1964 and is shown later that year. John Ingles; Jeff Wilson collection

Starch and other powdered and granular materials often travel in General American Airslide cars or pressure-differential covered hoppers. The cars' closed, pneumatic unloading systems result in less product waste (and mess) compared to standard covered hoppers. This 4,900-cf Airslide was built in 1993. J. David Ingles

Sodium chlorate, used to make chlorine dioxide on site at mills, is shipped in aluminum covered hoppers. This modern 3,621-cf car, built by Trinity, carries stenciling and a hazmat placard (UN 1495) for the material. J. David Ingles

Tank cars carrying LPG from the 1930s through the 1950s were distinctive. They were high-pressure cars, similar in design to chlorine cars, but larger (since LPG weighs much less than chlorine): 11,000 to 11,500 gallons. Cars to 20,000 gallons were operating by the early 1960s, and the coming of 100-ton cars after that led to the easily spotted 33,000-gallon cars of today — the largest tank cars on the rails.

Mills supplied by natural gas (which isn't shipped by rail) will be located near pipelines; in other words, in more heavily populated areas. This is most common in the East and Southeast.

When carried in bulk, lime — because of its density — usually rides in two-bay covered hoppers. This 3,281-cf car was built by Trinity in 2014 and is part of that company's lease fleet. Cody Grivno

CHAPTER NINE

PAPER-RELATED TRAIN OPERATIONS

Understanding how railroads and mills interact will greatly enhance a layout's realism. Our goal in modeling should be to go beyond moving random cars to and from a mill complex. Instead, the focus should be specific, such as delivering an inbound car of chlorine to the chemical receiving track, setting out two cars of coal on the power plant track, then pulling two boxcars of newsprint from warehouse track No. 2.

A Quebec Gatineau Railway local switches the Kruger Wayagamack paper mill at Trois-Rivières, Quebec, in 2015. The short line, owned by Genesee & Wyoming, operates the former Canadian Pacific line on which the mill is located. The excess-height boxcars are loaded with paper rolls. Dan Machalaba

How railroads handle pulpwood, wood chip, paper, and related traffic varies based on the size and type of a mill, the era, whether the railroad is a main line, branch, or short line, and whether there are other mills nearby. Modeling these operations can provide a great deal of interest on a layout, whether it is small or large.

Mill trackage

Even a small paper mill will require fairly extensive switching operations. Look at the overall number of tracks and see how many individual spotting areas there are. One mill may have separate spots for inbound pulpwood loads, inbound wood chip loads, inbound tank car loads, inbound covered hopper loads, inbound pulp bale loads, inbound fuel loads, and outbound paper loads — each of which may have spots for multiple cars. Multiple spots may be located on the same track, which will add to switching complexity.

Most mills have a small yard for receiving inbound cars, placing outbound cars, and temporarily storing cars until they're needed within the mill itself. This can be from two to four tracks (or more for large mills). This yard will be located between the mill trackage and the railroad serving it.

All mill and yard tracks will have a name — this follows standard railroad convention. Crews need to know specific locations: "that track over there" doesn't cut it; "Wood track 2" will be known by everyone. Chapter 10 provides some details on applying this to modeled situations.

The size of a mill will determine how switching moves are done, and by whom. Medium-size to large mills typically have an in-plant switcher or are switched by a mill-owned railroad (which may serve the mill itself with a nearby connection with another railroad). The serving railroad will drop off and pick up cuts of cars at the mill's yard, with the mill switcher then working the facility.

The mill railroad may, if it is a common carrier, be a shortline railroad that serves other local customers as well. Examples of this were the Berlin Mills Railway, a shortline owned by (and which served) the Brown Co. paper mill in Berlin, N.H. (from the 1970s to the 1990s), and the Minnesota, Dakota & Western, a grandly named four-mile shortline owned by Boise Cascade (until 2008) that served mills at International Falls, Minn.

A small mill may rely on local freight trains to do basic switching moves, and then move cars within the plant using car pullers, car movers, or rubber-tired switchers (tractors).

Atlanta & St. Andrews Bay provides switching services for the railroad's largest customer (and primary owner), International Paper, at Springfield, Fla. Here A&StAB GP7 No. 501 shoves a cut of tank cars at the massive mill in January 1975. Scott A. Hartley

In-mill operations

Mills generate significant traffic. A large mill will ship and receive dozens of cars every day. The railroad serving the mill will switch this traffic at least daily, and in some cases, twice each day. This can be done by a local (way) freight, which serves all customers along a stretch of railroad. If the traffic level warrants, a railroad may operate a "turn" strictly for that mill (or for area mills). This is a train that originates at a nearby yard and runs out-and-back to a dedicated customer or location.

Inbound daily mill traffic could include a couple dozen pulpwood and chip cars, a dozen or more Class A boxcar empties (for paper loads), several boxcar loads of market pulp or recycled paper, a tank car or two of chlorine, several other tank cars of clay slurry and assorted chemicals, a covered hopper of starch, and three or four coal cars (or tank cars of fuel oil or LPG). Outbound traffic will include empty pulp, chip, fuel, and chemical cars; boxcar loads of paper; and empty boxcars (pulp cars not suitable for paper loading).

Mills tend to be bunched together in many regions, so one rail line may serve multiple mills in a fairly short distance. The Milwaukee Road "Valley Line" in north-central Wisconsin, for example, served seven mills along its route. The local trains serving this stretch of railroad were much longer and more frequent than one that served a single mill — the "local" traffic might encompass more cars and more operations than seen on many secondary main lines.

Within a mill, the plant or shortline switcher will be continually working based on needs. A crew might start its shift by grabbing three empty paper boxcars from a yard track, moving them to a warehouse track, and swapping them for three loaded cars.

On the way back to the mill yard,

An Atlanta & St. Andrews Bay GP38-2 assembles a cut of empty tank cars into an outbound train at the mill yard at the International Paper Mill at Panama City, Fla., in July 1976. Robert E. Gabbey

the switcher pauses to grab a just-unloaded tank of titanium dioxide and two empty clay slurry cars, then pulls them to the yard and shoves them into the outbound track.

The switcher then goes to the power plant track, grabs two empty coal hoppers, and brings them to the yard. It then pulls three loaded coal hoppers and a boxcar load of market pulp and spots them at the appropriate tracks.

The local freight crew, in the meantime, has arrived at the mill yard with a couple dozen cars to drop off. It checks with the mill office to check the cars that need to be picked up, pulls them from the appropriate yard tracks, and shoves its setouts to the yard.

Operations continue in similar fashion throughout the shift, which can easily keep an operator or two busy for hours.

Challenges for operators (prototype as well as model) include tight spaces; there may only be enough room on one track for the locomotive and a few cars, requiring multiple moves to swap loads for empties or to bring cars back and forth to the mill yard. Small industrial locomotives may be limited to pulling one or two loaded cars at a time.

Operators have to be aware of clearance issues — a 60-foot excess-height

The Wisconsin Great Northern in 1997 took over a former Canadian National branch in northern Wisconsin that serves two paper mills. In December 2015 a WGN freight carries pulpwood loads that were transloaded from trucks in Hayward to the Domtar mill in Nekoosa and Ahlstrom's Thilmany mill in Kaukauna. Steve Smedley

Several slurry, starch, and clay tank cars and covered hoppers wait on holding tracks at Appleton Papers in Kaukauna, Wis., in this 1990s scene, while several boxcars await loading on a warehouse track at right. Jim Hediger

A Cloquet Terminal Railroad crew switches the wood yard at the Sappi mill in Cloquet, Minn., in March 2024. Mill and rail operations continue year-round regardless of weather. Steve Smedley

Some mill tracks have clearance issues — excess-height boxcars won't clear the overhead awning on the warehouse building at left at Wisconsin's Appleton Papers. The indoor track at right may provide additional clearance, but tight curves sometimes preclude moving long cars (such as modern 60-foot excess-height boxcars). Jim Hediger

boxcar, for example, may fit on one warehouse track but not another, or excess-height cars may not fit on tracks inside of buildings. Some tracks may require precise spotting at doors or unloading connection points. Crews may also have to be aware of blocking in-plant roadways and lots, so may be limited in the number of cars they can pull at one time (or the amount of time they can be stationary in some locations).

Cars with employees on them (being loaded or unloaded) will be "blue flagged" — the car or track will be tagged with a blue marker indicating they are not to be moved. Switch crews need to work around these cars while moving others.

Train operations

Railroads serving mills handled a lot of pulpwood and wood chip traffic into the 1960s. Hauls were usually relatively short — a couple hundred miles, sometimes longer for chips — because of mills' locations near their source trees. (For example, a pulpwood rack wouldn't be loaded in South Carolina and sent to a mill in Maine.) Trucks originally carried only short-haul traffic, but by the 1960s they were taking longer-distance traffic as well; today most pulp logs travel by semi.

A key in handling pulpwood cars, especially V-deck racks, is train speed. As Chapter 6 noted, loads were prone to shifting and tipping, so railroads imposed speed limits as low as 25 or 30 mph. This means a railroad can't just couple a cut of pulpwood loads at the rear of a hotshot or secondary freight, as a train that would otherwise be able to do 50 would then be stuck with the lower speed limit. This means these loads were almost always carried on slow-speed local freights.

Other raw materials heading to a mill can travel long distances. Tank cars of clay slurry from Georgia or chlorine from upstate New York, for example, might travel a thousand or more miles to a mill in the Midwest or West, traveling along main lines that serve no mills.

Paper loads in boxcars are often largely indistinguishable from any other cars (although Chapter 5 shows examples of dedicated paper cars). They're handled in regular freight trains: riding in a local to the nearest classification yard, then in mainline through freights to a yard near the final customer, where a local freight again takes charge of the car or cars, making the final delivery.

A challenge for railroads is limiting cycle times, getting the empty boxcars back to mills for loading as quickly as possible.

Paper customers

Modeling a mill customer is another way to get paper mill traffic on a layout. For newsprint this can mean a metropolitan daily paper, a printing company or, for packaged goods, a distribution warehouse for a wholesaler or store chain. For customers not located directly on a rail line, a railroad will deliver the car to a team track or a designated transload facility. This was fairly common for large-city newspapers, which were often located in downtown buildings that weren't in industrial (track-served) areas.

An example on page 101 shows a Milwaukee operation where boxcars of newsprint rolls were off-loaded at a covered dock and transferred to open-bed trucks owned by the *Milwaukee Journal.* Modeling such a facility would be an interesting detail, providing a chance to see paper rolls outside of a car (leaving no doubt as to the boxcars' contents) with details such as a forklift, truck, and workers.

A large printing company may receive multiple cars at once. The photo atop page 100 shows a mid-2010s example at a Quad/Graphics printing plant in Wisconsin. The company at the time received about 1,900 carloads of paper a year. Although the tracks at the plant are a simple arrangement, serving railroads may provide custom switching arrangements, storage at nearby yards, or priority switching for special paper shipments.

A printing plant like this may have provided outbound loads of finished products during the steam and early diesel eras, but by the 1960s almost all outbound traffic would be by truck.

A Duluth & Northeastern freight drifts downgrade across state highway 33 near Cloquet, Minn., in 1954 as a pulpwood truck waits at the crossing. Pulpwood and coal loads are at the head end. Franklin A. King

Southern Railway high-nose GP30 No. 2578 leads a local train heavy with pulpwood cars at at Oxford-Henderson Junction (Oxford, N.C.). The train is leaving Oxford, bound for Keysville, Va. Curt Tillotson, Jr.

Maine Central GP7 572, repainted in the railroad's original 1950s scheme, leads a train with a mix of pulpwood cars of different styles at Waterville, Maine, in January 1979. Francis J. DiFalco

Printing plants are common customers for paper boxcars and are good subjects for modeling. This is Quad/Graphics in Waukesha, Wis., in the mid-1990s. Note how the boxcars have been uncoupled to enable spotting at individual doors. Not only does this complicate switching — it can also limit the type and length of cars received at the plant.
Jim Hediger

A Union Pacific local drops off five loaded boxcars inside the warehouse at the International Paper container plant at Lincoln, Ill., in January 2024. The very modelable complex receives cardboard made at other International mills and converts it to containers for various customers.
Steve Smedley

At Trois-Rivières, Quebec, the Quebec Gatineau Railway provides wood chip transloading service for the nearby Kruger Wayagamack paper mill. Chip cars are spotted on a long track at a yard. A loader then transfers chips to trucks for the trip to the nearby mill. Other inbound loads are handled in similar fashion. Dan Machalaba

Through the 1980s, the Milwaukee Road served this newsprint transload center on the north side of Milwaukee (along the road's famous "Beer Line" branch). Boxcars brought in newsprint; a forklift pulled the rolls and moved them into storage, then onto trucks for the *Milwaukee Journal* newspaper. The Milwaukee Road boxcar in the middle photo has stenciling indicating it is in assigned service. These photos are from 1980. Three photos: Richard Cecil

CHAPTER TEN

MODELING PAPER MILLS

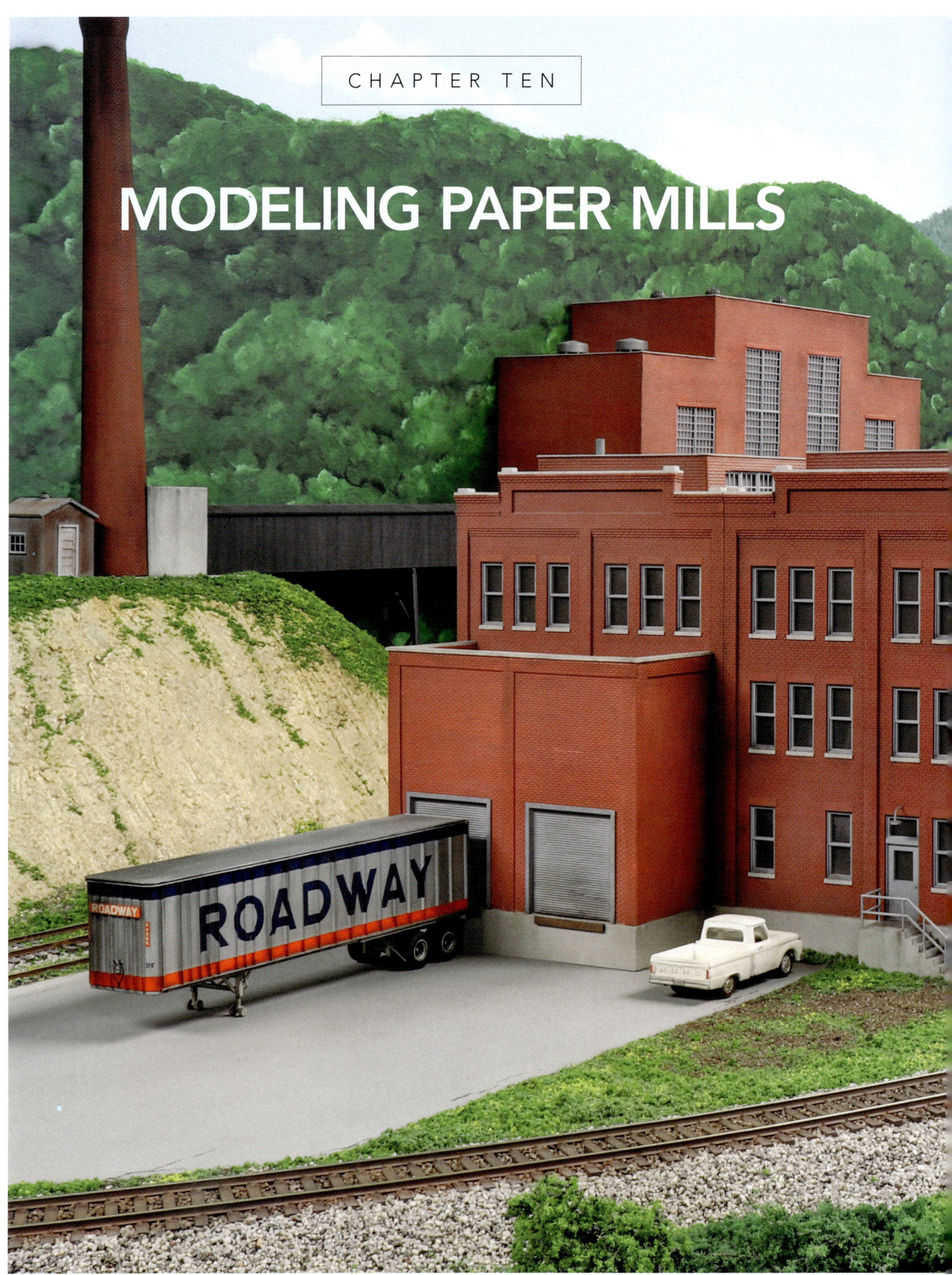

Paper mills — even by the early 1900s — were huge operations covering many acres. It is virtually impossible to model a complete mill to scale, even in N, and even if the mill itself is the layout. There are, however, many ways to use selective compression to focus your modeling efforts on the key features of a mill and to realistically capture a prototype mill's operating potential.

Joe Green built this large paper mill complex on his 1974-era HO scale Chesapeake & Ohio, a 30x31-foot basement layout. Joe combined a variety of model structure kits as flats and 3-D buildings to create Back Creek Paper (based on a prototype Westvaco mill). Here a C&O U23B leads a local with boxcars, chemical cars, and wood chip loads bound for the mill. At left and in the distance, boxcars, tank cars, and covered hoppers await loading and unloading on the various mill tracks. Joe Green

Paper mills are huge complexes, so selective compression is needed to model them. The Georgia-Pacific mill at Crossett, Ark., has two paper machines: The dark-roofed building in the foreground is a tissue mill; the long white building above it is a paper mill. Pulp processing is at the center. Railroad tracks wind throughout the complex. Georgia-Pacific

We'll look at what a mill's primary features are (in terms of railroad service), examine ways of compressing buildings and other features to fit available spaces, and then we'll list some models that have been produced. We'll also show a couple of track plans that will hopefully provide hands-on ideas you can apply to your own layout.

Selective compression

What is selective compression? In modeling, it's the art of taking a large structure or detail from real life and shrinking it, while keeping the features and characteristics that make it "modelable." At the same time, we can minimize or eliminate buildings and features that don't add to our modeling goals. Wisely using selective compression is a key, even if you have a lot of space.

As an example: For modeling a mill, we can focus on the buildings and areas that are the most distinctive and have tracks serving them: the warehouse, power plant, chemical storage area/tanks, and wood storage (all rail served), plus the digester and paper-making buildings, as they're distinctive and prominent at prototype mills. To save space, we can just pretend that features such as the lime kiln, water treatment plant, employee parking lots, and administrative offices are out of sight behind other buildings.

To put this into modeling perspective: A building housing a paper machine at a prototype mill might be 500 feet long. This translates to more than 5½ feet in HO scale and just over 3 feet in N scale — and that's just one building in the mill complex. Selective compression means shortening the building by a foot or two, yet leaving it large enough that it still dominates a scene. At the same time it can be kept as a low-relief flat along a backdrop so it takes up little actual area on a layout.

However, you still need to devote significant space to make a paper mill believable. You need more than a couple of buildings with a track or two for boxcars and a spur for a tank car. If space is really tight, consider another business related to the industry: a wood-loading yard, printing company, or packaging company are all simpler, but allow paper traffic in a relatively small area. Or you can model just the mill's receiving yard, with the mill perhaps as a photo on the backdrop behind a ridge or fence.

Models

A number of model manufacturers have offered structures suitable for paper mill buildings. Look at the models themselves, and not their labels — a structure kit labeled as a factory of some other type might be perfect for a mill building.

Also, understand that many models have been offered in limited runs, and some haven't been produced in years. Most of these can still be found if you do some digging online (eBay is a great place to start). If it's been produced, you can almost guarantee that there's still one out there somewhere for sale.

For the main mill buildings, a great start is the series of structures from the Walthers Superior Paper series in HO and N (walthers.com); although out of production, they can still be found online through eBay and other dealers. Buildings include a rolling mill, boiler/recovery building, concrete pulp tanks, and warehouse with door opening for railcars. Walthers has also offered power plants in modern steel (Lakefront Energy) and older brick (Northern Light & Power) versions, including a substation and related details, that are good representations of power plants at mills. For a coal-powered plant, Walthers offers a coal trestle in HO.

Walthers and Design Preservation Models (now a division of Woodland Scenics, woodlandscenics.com) have offered a number of brick industrial-style buildings and modular wall sections that would be appropriate for mills through the mid-1900s. Walthers also has (in HO and N) a kit for a prefab concrete-wall warehouse, the Modern Concrete Grocery Warehouse, that would fit right in as a warehouse building in a modern mill.

Rix Products/Pikestuff (www.rixproducts.com) also has produced several industrial building kits in prefab metal style suitable for mills from the early diesel era to the present. Walthers offers similar kits in N and HO scales, and ITLA Scale Models has wall systems and modules in HO (itlascalemodels.com).

Plastruct (plastruct.com) is a great source for tanks, piping, and framework in all scales. Other good sources of tanks and details include Walthers, Faller, Piko, and Kibri. Oil refinery kits from Walthers and Plastruct can be great sources for the tanks, piping, and associated details found at any chemical-process mill.

Details such as ladders and walkways have been made by Alkem Scale Models (alkemscalemodels.biz), Gold Medal Models (out of business), Tichy (tichytraingroup.com), and Walthers.

A modeling tip with tanks: Don't look at the listed scale on the model. Instead, rely on the overall size — HO tanks often work well for N scale, and N tanks are great for small tanks in HO. Set the scale by using ladders, platforms, and walkways on the tanks in the scale you're modeling.

Wood chip piles can be simulated with foam board carved to shape, then covered with sawdust glued in place. Paint the pile with a color close to that of your sawdust; you can use the paint or thinned white glue or matte medium (which dries flat) to hold the sawdust in place.

Pulpwood logs can be modeled with real twigs. Conifer twigs, gathered late in the fall, work well; use a diameter to match your scale. A wire cutter will make quick work of cutting them to needed lengths. If you do this, a couple of handy tips: First, bake them to kill any insects or mold that might be lurking within — an hour at 200 degrees or so should do the trick. When the twigs have cooled, give them a dip in a mix of thinned matte medium (one

This 1998 view of the Crown Vantage (former Brown Co.) pulp mill in Berlin, N.H., shows old-style brick construction, with a dominating smokestack. Study walls, windows, and other features of prototype mills when looking at potential models and kits — modular walls would be a good option for this mill. Marty McGuirk

This metal-roofed, concrete-block warehouse is at Champion Paper in Hamilton, Ohio. The 1990s scene includes a pair of former Conrail boxcars owned by shortline Great Miami & Scioto Railway. Features such as the tightly-curved tracks and turnout; crumbling poured-concrete dock; uneven, cracked paved surfaces; and fire hydrant with protective barriers all offer interesting modeling potential. Jim Hediger

The nature of the long, low structures of many mills lends them to re-creating in model form with a combination of backdrop photos and building flats. This is the International Paper Co. mill in Panama City, Fla., in the 1970s. Panama City Chamber of Commerce

part matte medium to four or five parts water). This will seal them and keep future insects from deciding to take up residence. The matte medium will be invisible once it dries (white glue can leave a bit of a shine). Place them on waxed paper until dry.

Small stacks can simply be glued in place twig by twig. For large piles, cut a form from foam board as with a chip pile, then glue the twigs in place over the form.

Mill layout and planning

The extent of what can and should be included in a model of a mill largely depends on your available space. Key elements to include are the structures and details directly served by tracks: the chip and pulpwood storage areas, warehouse (open or with tracks going into the building), power plant (if it receives coal, fuel oil, or LPG), and the tank car and covered hopper loading/unloading areas or buildings.

The truck shipping area of a warehouse, although impressive (and large, especially at modern mills), may be best left to imagination — on the opposite side of the warehouse, out of sight. However, if you like truck and trailer models, by all means find room for part of a dock to show off your models.

The lime kiln, although vital in many mills, can be out of sight behind another building as it is not directly rail served. The water treatment plant is another feature that can usually be omitted on a modeled mill.

The use of building flats and backdrop images is a key in conserving space while increasing the apparent size of a mill. Good examples for this are the digester building and tanks, because of their height and dominance in scenes, and the buildings housing the paper machines, because they are long and prominent.

Features such as warehouses or chip/wood piles can be combinations of flats and three-dimensional models. Examples could include a warehouse as a flat, but with a partial building with loading dock (or track entering a door) extending from the flat, or a pulp- or chip-unloading track with a small pile of logs or chips next to a backdrop, with a photo of a larger pile on the backdrop.

For photos on a backdrop: If you're not able to take images yourself, check for photos online (you can use images you find for your personal use). A good starting point is the Library of Congress photo repository (www.loc.gov/pictures/). It's beyond the scope of this book, but by using Photoshop or other photography or graphics software, you can resize images, change angles, and combine photos, then print them out and glue them to a backdrop.

Depending upon your space, you can also use the backdrop to conceal tracks passing through it. Examples would be an opening into a warehouse or a chemical-unloading building on the backdrop, with tracks extending a couple of carlengths behind the backdrop.

Look for features to add to a backdrop with photos. Chip and wood piles, like this one at the Sappi paper mill in Cloquet, Minn., in 2019, are good candidates. The Cloquet Terminal, which switches the mill, is a successor to the Duluth & Northeastern; the MP15 is an ex-Union Pacific engine. David C. Schauer

Wood construction was rare for mill buildings after 1900, and those that existed usually didn't last long. This mill at Lincoln, N.H., in 1939 is an exception, and still had some wood clapboard structures. Marion Post Wolcott, Library of Congress

Trackwork

Mills generally have yards to store cars, with the railroad serving the mill dropping off and picking up large blocks of cars (often entire trains). The mill switcher (or shortline or industrial railroad serving the mill) then does in-plant switching, pulling and spotting cars, as Chapter 9 explains. You can model this even with a simple two-track stub-ended yard, with one track designated for setouts and one for pickups; including an extra track or two will expand your operational possibilities.

As you plan the trackwork and lay out the mill itself, remember to keep all tracks within easy reach for operations (uncoupling, rerailing cars, cleaning). A 24" depth is usually quite workable, while 30" becomes a long stretch for most people. Remember

The warehouse and other brick structures at Menasha Corporation's Otsego, Mich., mill, feature a more modern curtain-style brick construction compared to the mill on page 105. The mill, shown in the 1990s and now closed, specialized in food-grade corrugated cardboard. Jim Hediger

Areas where tracks wind between buildings and tanks are fascinating, but in modeling, make sure you allow room for track maintenance and rerailing access. This is the tank car unloading area at Appleton Papers in Kaukauna, Wis., in the 1990s. Jim Hediger

that the taller the layout, the more difficult it becomes to reach across a shelf.

You can get ideas for laying out the mill and trackwork from looking at photos of prototype mills (seen throughout this book) and from the track plans on pages 110 and 111. Be aware, however, that although tracks that wind around and through tall buildings and behind tanks and other details look great (and are quite realistic), they can be difficult to access on a model railroad. Make sure you have clear access to all tracks, and that an arm reaching into a scene to throw a turnout or rerail a car won't accidentally damage structures and details.

Since in-plant trackwork is all slow-speed, you can get away with tight curves and sharp turnouts (No. 4), and you can use wye turnouts and crossings of various angles as needed. Make sure that the freight cars you plan to run will work on the curves. A radius of 18" in HO or 9¾" in N will work for older eras where 40- and 50-foot cars were standard. For modern plants with 60-foot boxcars and 60- and 70-foot chip cars, test some models and see what works well.

You'll find a couple of sample track plans from Jim Hediger and Joe Green on the following pages. Both could be used as-is to create a stand-alone layout based entirely on mill operations; either could also be modified to add a mill to a larger layout.

In both cases the designers had a specific era and region in mind, but you can easily adapt either to suit mills in many eras and locations. Think of them as starting points, then modify them based on your own ideas and prototype interests.

Details

The drives, roads, truck loading areas, parking areas, and paths within mills were originally gravel and dirt, but they largely gave way to paved asphalt and concrete areas by the 1950s and later. The surrounding ground itself varies by region, as prototype photos show.

Signs are an important scenic element. You'll find warning signs for clearances, chemical hazards, and materials, and roadway control signs and signals along driveways (especially where they cross tracks). Buildings, doors, docks, and storage tanks will be labeled with numbers and names.

The name of the paper company is often prominently featured with large signs on one or more buildings or on

Trucks and other vehicles can help set the era and region, and sometimes the specific prototype. There's no doubt who owns this mill. The prefab metal warehouse has signs indicating doors along the truck dock. Jim Hediger

This 1960 scene is at the Scott Paper mill in Everett, Wash., on the Great Northern. The track with tight curves and multiple crossings, the track in pavement, fences, gates, and other details deserve careful modeling. The GN served and provided switching at the mill multiple times every day. Brotherhood of Locomotive Firemen and Enginemen

Jim Hediger taped together the walls of the Walthers HO mill to make this mockup, seeing how the pieces could be used as flats along a backdrop. The squat tank and blue building are additional kits from Rix. Jim Hediger

the smokestack. Additional signs are often located at the street or highway entrances. Tall water towers (the same type used in cities and towns for municipal water) are prominent, and often bear the corporate name and logo (Walthers has modern and classic water towers in HO and N).

By the 1960s, mills — especially those in and near cities — were surrounded by fences, often chain-link topped with barbed or razor wire. Vehicle access for modern plants is at controlled gates with full-time security or electronic key/pass gates, with all vehicles checking in (usually with separate gates for commercial vehicles and employees). Entry gates often cross railroad tracks entering the plant. Scale fences are made by Alkem Scale Models, Motrak Models, Walthers, Woodland Scenics, and others.

Fire control is paramount at mills. Modern plants will have outdoor hydrants located throughout the grounds, along with sprinkler systems throughout all buildings. Exterior piping routes water to chip and log piles to keep them wet.

Mills use a tremendous amount of electricity. Along with inbound high-voltage lines, most plants will have a small substation on the grounds, with fencing surrounding the transformers and high-voltage electrical gear. Walthers has offered substation kits in HO and N scales.

Important support equipment includes forklifts, cranes, loaders, hoists, tractors, bulldozers, and conveyors. Several manufacturers offer suitable models, including Artitec, Atlas, Diecast Masters, Eko, Kibri, Piko, Walthers, and Woodland Scenics. Vehicles are also important, as autos, trucks, and trailers can help set the era and region, aided by specific names on trailers (local trucking companies or the paper company). Pickup trucks and other work trucks will be found throughout the plant.

And, of course no mill scene would be complete without figures to bring it to life. Mills are active places, with workers on loading docks, on and near vehicles and heavy equipment, at the wood yard, and throughout the plant. The figures can help place the era, both in dress and color as well as equipment (hard hats at modern plants, for example).

GORDON PAPER CO. IN HO

This HO plan, developed by Jim Hediger, is designed to fit on a 4x8-foot sheet of plywood with one corner cut away and flipped. It can easily be adapted to smaller scales, used as-is for a table-style layout, or it can be modified and added to a larger layout.

Jim intended the plan to represent a generic 1990s-era mill located in northern Wisconsin and served by the Wisconsin Central. It has sharp curves and small turnouts, which — like some prototype mills — will limit the size and length of rolling stock used.

In simulating modeled operations, Jim planned that the mill would produce daily traffic of 10 to 12 carloads of finished paper outbound, with daily inbound loads including 10 to 12 loads of wood chips, two tank cars of clay slurry, and a covered hopper of starch. Additional traffic could include inbound boxcars of market pulp or recycled paper and a car or two of chemicals or additional additives per day (including chlorine, caustic soda, hydrogen peroxide, and titanium dioxide). Depending upon the fuel being used, a car or two of coal, fuel oil, or LPG would be appropriate, with an occasional outbound tank car of turpentine or alcohol.

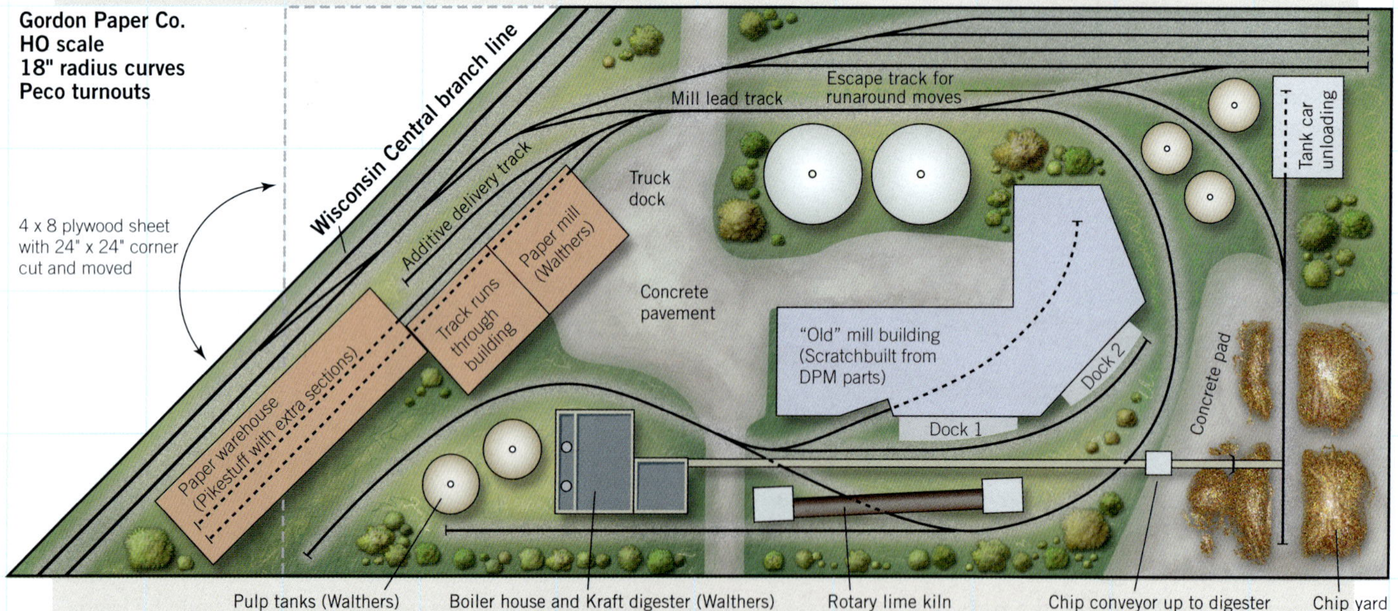

ROOM-SIZED MILL LAYOUT IN HO

Joe Green developed this track plan for a paper mill, made to fit a 10x14-foot room in HO scale. The plan could easily be adapted to N scale as well, either in a smaller space or by increasing the relative size of the mill and amount of trackage. Elements of the plan can also be taken and applied to a larger layout.

Joe developed the plan for the mill — which he calls Back Creek Paper — based on his large home layout, which features the mill shown on page 102. The full story on how he developed the plan, along with additional photos of the mill on his home layout, is in the October 2023 *Model Railroader*. A full story on his C&O Ryder Gap Subdivision layout was featured in *Model Railroad Planning 2021*.

Pulp Mill
Track 1
Track 2
Track 3
Track 4
Track 5
Track 6
Track 7
Track 8
Main track
West Va. Pulp & Paper Co.
COVINGTON, VA.
Woodyard
Track 9
Track 10
Track 11
Milepost 1
Milepost 2
West

1937 Westvaco pulp mill track diagram
Based on drawings from Chesapeake & Ohio Historical Society
Not to scale

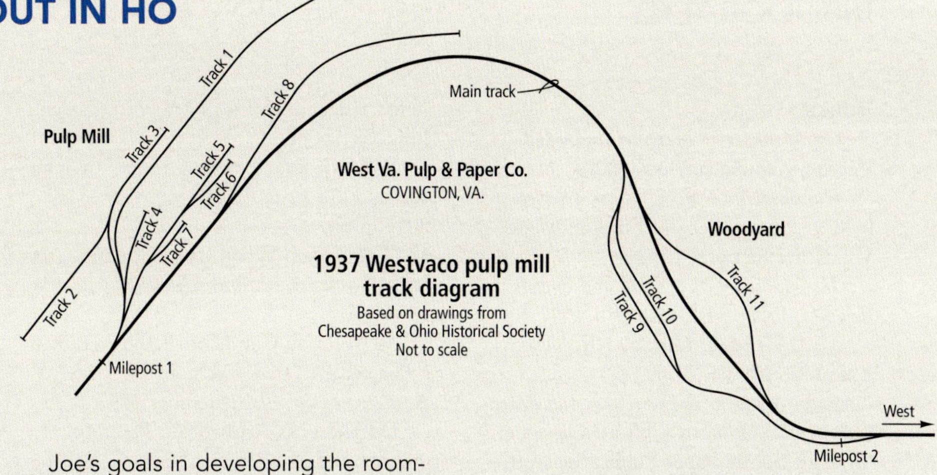

Joe's goals in developing the room-size plan were to create a "what-if" scenario if he had to move to a smaller space. He wanted to retain the appearance and feel of a large prototype mill, while providing enough potential for a two- to three-hour operating session for a single crew.

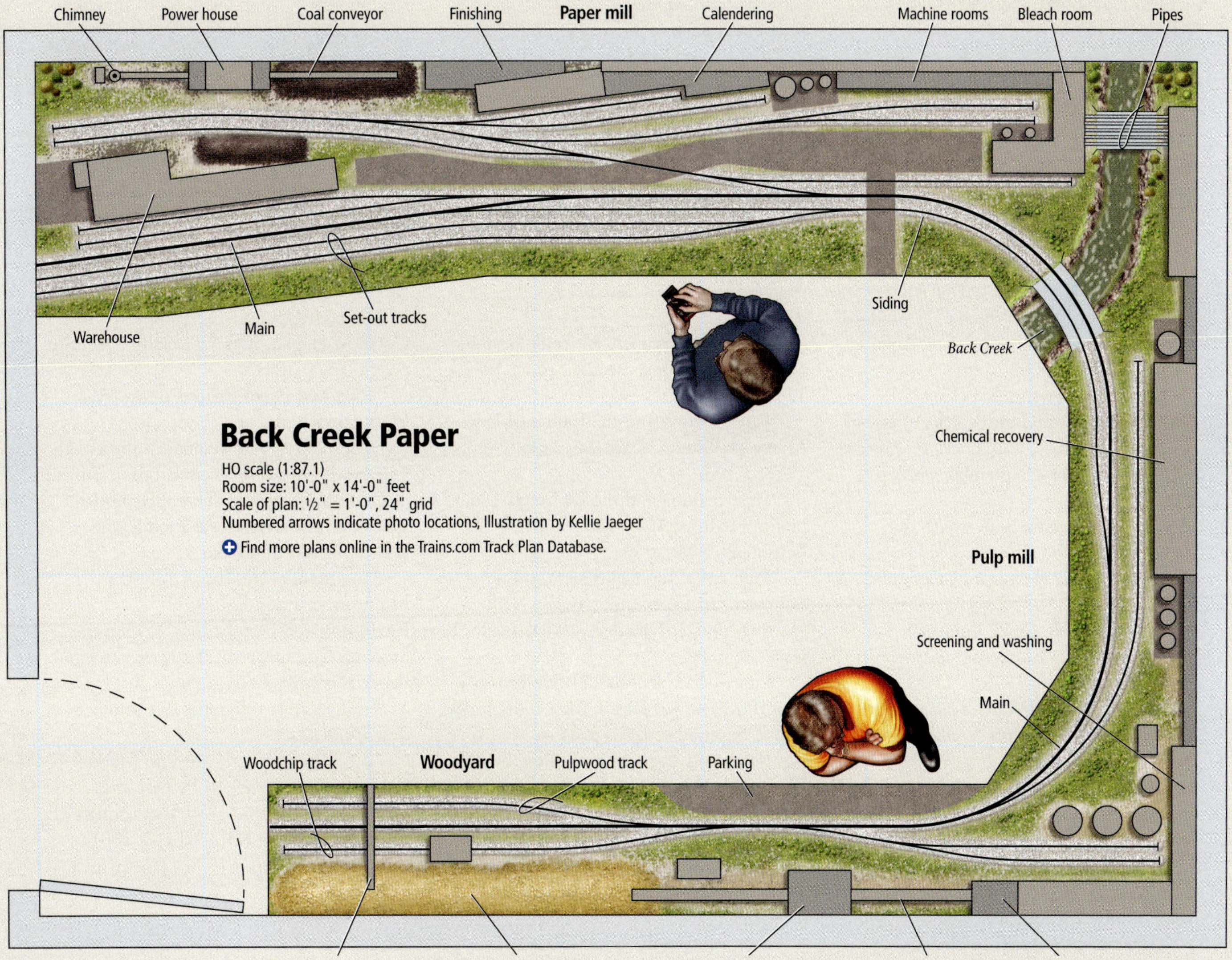

Chimney
Power house
Coal conveyor
Finishing
Paper mill
Calendering
Machine rooms
Bleach room
Pipes
Warehouse
Main
Set-out tracks
Siding
Back Creek
Chemical recovery
Pulp mill
Screening and washing
Main
Woodchip track
Woodyard
Pulpwood track
Parking

Back Creek Paper
HO scale (1:87.1)
Room size: 10'-0" x 14'-0" feet
Scale of plan: ½" = 1'-0", 24" grid
Numbered arrows indicate photo locations, Illustration by Kellie Jaeger
Find more plans online in the Trains.com Track Plan Database.

BIBLIOGRAPHY

Books

Commodities by Freight Car, by Jeff Wilson. Kalmbach Media, 2023

Handbook for Pulp & Paper Technologists, by G.A. Snook, Second Edition. Angus Wilde Productions, 1992.

The Manufacture of Pulp and Paper, Second Edition. McGraw-Hill, 1927.

Modern Freight Cars, by Jeff Wilson. Kalmbach Media, 2019.

Paper Matters: Today's Paper and Board Industry Unfolded, by Clifford Lines and Graham Booth. Paper Publications Ltd., 1990.

Pollution Control and Chemical Recovery in the Pulp and Paper Industry, by H.R. Jones. Noyes Data Corporation, 1973.

Transport and Handling in the Pulp and Paper Industry, Vol. 1, edited by Leonard E. Haas and John E. Kalish. Miller Freeman Publications, 1975.

Wisconsin Central: Railroad Success Story, by Otto P. Dobnick and Steve Glischinski. Kalmbach, 1997.

Periodicals

"American-Canadian Newsprint Paper Industry and the Tariff," by Constant Southworth, *Journal of Political Economy,* October 1922, p. 681.

"Atlantic Coast Line W-4 Pulpwood Car," by James Kinkaid, *Railroad Model Craftsman,* September 2021, p. 46.

"Canadian National's 1937 AAR-Design 40-Foot Steel Boxcars," by Stafford Swain, *Railroad Model Craftsman,* August 1993, p. 81.

"Canadian Newsprint, 1913-1930: National Policies and the North American Economy," by Trevor J.O. Dick, *The Journal of Economic History,* September 1982, p. 659.

"Canadian Pacific Railway 70-Ton, 50-Foot Plug-Door Boxcars," by J.A. Chambers, *Model Railroading,* December 1989, p. 34.

"CP Rail's Side-Stake Pulpwood Flatcar," by Keith Thompson, *Model Railroader,* February 1996, p. 121.

"Freight on 4%" (Watco's Blue Ridge Southern), by Jim Wrinn, *Trains,* December 2016, p. 52.

"General Steel Castings Pulpwood Car," by James Kinkaid, *Railroad Model Craftsman,* August 2015, p. 60.

"GN's Gunderson Wood Chip Gondolas," by James Kinkaid, *Mainline Modeler,* June 2004, p. 22.

"Greenville Wood Chip Hopper," by James Kinkaid, *Railroad Model Craftsman,* July 2021, p. 46.

"GSI 45-Foot Pulpwood Flat," by James Kinkaid, *Railroad Model Craftsman,* May 2017, p. 64.

"Gunderson Wood Chip Gondolas," by James Kinkaid, *Mainline Modeler,* May 2004, p. 37.

"A Mill You Can Model: The Action at a Paper Plant" by J. Emmons Lancaster, *RailModel Journal,* September 1997, p. 11.

"Minnesota's Arrowhead: Taconite, Timber, and Tourism" by David C. Schauer, *Trains,* August 2021, p. 20.

"Modeling a Modern Paper Mill," by Bernard Kempinski, *Model Railroader,* April 2002, p. 84

"Modeling the Paper Industry: Railroad-Served Paper Sites," by J. Emmons Lancaster, *RailModel Journal,* September 1997, p. 17.

"Newsprint Boxcars" (NSC 50-foot cars), by John Riddell, *Model Railroader,* June 2002, p. 70.

"The Paper Chase," by Barry Biglow, *CN Lines* (Canadian National Railways Historical Assn.), Vol. 18, No. 2, p. 5.

"The Paper Revolution," by John Studeny, *Proceedings of the Pennsylvania Academy of Science,* Vol. 41 (1967), p. 230.

"Paper Trail," by Dan Machalaba, *Trains,* November 2015, p. 62.

"The Paper Train: 1," by Tony Hodun, *Freight Cars Journal,* No. 21, Winter 1987, p. 14.

"The Paper Train: 2," by Tony Hodun, *Freight Cars Journal,* No. 22, Spring 1987, p. 12

"Papermaking and the Railroads," by Marty McGuirk, *Model Railroader,* October 1998, p. 100.

"Papermaking and the Railroads Today," by Jim Hediger, *Model Railroader,* November 1998, p. 90.

"Pulp and Chip Equipment in the Southeastern Paper Industry," by Neill Herring, *Freight Cars Journal,* Vol. 6, No. 2, Issue 30, p. 16.

"Pulpwood Cars," by D.P. Holbrook, *RailModel Journal.* Part 4, May 1990, p. 48; Part 7, September 1991, p. 24

"Pulpwood, Part 2: The Rolling Stock Used by the North Central Roads," by D.P. Holbrook, *RailModel Journal,* January 1990, p. 54.

"Pulpwood, Part 3: The Superwood Plant," *RailModel Journal,* Febrary 1990, p. 44.

"Pulpwood in the South, Part 1: The V-Deck Woodrack Cars," by Rhett Coates, *RailModel Journal,* September 1993, p. 27.

"Pulpwood in the South, Part 2: Operations on the Seaboard Line," by Larry Denton, *RailModel Journal,* October 1993, p. 4.

"Pulpwood Trains Can Be Profitable," by John G. Kneiling, *Trains,* March 1975, p. 26.

"The Rise and Fall of the Canadian Pulp and Paper Sector," by Bryan E.C. Bogdanski, *The Forestry Chronicle,* November/December 2014, p. 785.

"A Rural Wood Chip Plant," by Kyle Lael, *Model Railroader,* October 2002, p. 96.

"Seaboard System Wood Chip Hopper Fleet," by Eric A. Neubauer, *Freight Cars Journal,* Vol. 6, No. 2, Issue 30, p. 19.

Miscellaneous

Association of American Railroads (aar.org), various fact sheets, statistics summaries, and car loading instructions/diagrams

Car and Locomotive Cyclopedia, Simmons-Boardman, various editions

Field Guide to Tank Cars, Fourth Edition, Association of American Railroads, 2022.

"Getting the wood out," by Bill Cook, Michigan State University Extension paper, July 2019.

Greenbrier Companies (gbrx.com), product descriptions

Official Railway Equipment Register, various issues

"Logs, sticks, bolts, and chips," by Bill Cook, Michigan State University Extension paper, January 2015.

"Pulp and Paper Policies of the War Production Board and Predecessor Agencies, May 1940 to January 1944." U.S. Civilian Production Administration Bureau of Demobilization; Historical Reports on War Administration: War Production Board, Special Study No. 7.

"The State of the Paper Industry: Monitoring the Indicators of Environmental Performance." Paper; the Steering Committee of the Environmental Paper Network, 2007.

TrinityRail (trinityrail.com), product descriptions

"U.S. Paper, Paperboard, and Market Pulp Capacity Trends by Process and Location, 1970-2000." U.S. Department of Agriculture, paper FPL-RP-602, 2001.